W9-BKE-148

3 1951 00140 1774

AMERICAN POTTERS

AMERICAN POTTERS

THE WORK OF TWENTY MODERN MASTERS □ BY GARTH CLARK

WATSON-GUPTILL PUBLICATIONS / NEW YORK

First published 1981 in the United States and Canada by Watson-Guptill Publications,
a division of Billboard Publications, Inc.,
1515 Broadway, New York, N.Y. 10036

Library of Congress Cataloging in Publication Data
Clark, Garth.
  American potters.
  Bibliography: p.
  Includes index.
  1. Pottery, American.   2. Pottery—20th century—
United States.   3. Potters—United States—Biography.
I. Title.
NK4008.C5   1981   738'.092'2 [B]   80-28628

ISBN 0-8230-0213-6   1/94 GIFT

First Printing, 1981

PHOTOGRAPHIC CREDITS

*Except for the following, all
photographs are by Terry A. Collins.*

Ryusei Arita, page 53
Richard Baume, pages 132, 133
Frank Beader, pages 108, 109, 110
Lee Fatherree, pages 124, 125, 126, 127
Jane Courtney Frisse, page 20
Rena Hansen, page 43
Robert G. Harvey, pages 68, 69, 71
Sue McGraw, pages 134, 135
Michael McTwigan, pages 65, 84, 85
George Meinzinger, pages 24, 28, 128,
  129, 130, 131
Lester Mertz, page 120
Thatcher Nagle, page 45
Joe Schopplein, pages 94, 95
Dick Schwarze, pages 112, 113
Garry Sutton, page 73
Bob Vigiletti, page 42
Tony Vinella, pages 96, 97, 98, 99

ACKNOWLEDGMENTS

In December 1978, just as the outline for this book was being developed, I received an invitation to be guest curator of an exhibition for the Gallery of Art, University of Northern Iowa. The exhibition, titled "The Contemporary American Potter," featured sixteen of the twenty artists represented here, and after opening at the Gallery of Art (April 28, 1980), it began a two-year tour under the auspices of the Smithsonian Institution Traveling Exhibition Service (SITES). The projects grew closely together, and I would like to thank those associated with the exhibition for providing encouragement and some of the resources necessary to undertake this book: to Barbara Cassino for suggesting the project, Sanford Sivitz Shaman for organizing the exhibition, Betty Teller of SITES, photographer Terry Collins, the Driscoll Foundation of St. Paul, Minnesota, the Iowa Arts Council, and the National Endowment for the Arts. In addition, I am grateful to my assistant Mark Del Vecchio, Lynne Wagner, George Meinzinger, Helen Williams Drutt, Rena Bransten, Alice Westphal, and all those who have contributed to this project. A special debt of thanks goes to my editor, Michael McTwigan, for his objectivity and patience, and to Jay Anning for his sensitive design. Last, this book is dedicated to the twenty artists it celebrates and to Barbara Cassino for setting the ball in motion.

Garth Clark
Los Angeles

CONTENTS

INTRODUCTION

Ceramics, like the other mediums of the "craft" genre, has long been relegated to a subordinate position among the arts, as is indicated by its classification as a "minor" or "decorative" art by Western historians and critics. Perhaps because of its humble material, or the utilitarian purpose that caused its invention, the pot has been regarded as an unfit genre for the highest forms of artistic expression—except by potters themselves, of course. For despite prejudice and neglect, twentieth-century ceramists have been surely and steadily shaping and reshaping their medium into one of the most vital forms of modern artistic expression.

The appearance of this book is therefore especially meaningful. It is the first critical study of the American potter's role in modern art, the first attempt to understand one of art's most misunderstood mediums. In *American Potters* Garth Clark surveys the nation's leading vessel makers, who for the past three decades have been mentors and teachers to an entire generation of ceramists. It would seem to be no coincidence that America's potters have become the world's leaders in clay at the same moment its painters and sculptors have come to the forefront in their mediums.

The potters represented here hold a variety of attitudes toward their work: some regard it as everyday, utilitarian ware; others consider each piece precious and irreplaceable. Despite their very different perceptions, these artists all evince a thoroughgoing devotion to their medium. Equal to their commitment to clay—perhaps even greater—is their reverence for the vessel. Even when many ceramists themselves abandoned the vessel in search of new forms, these potters continued their exploration of its possibilities. *American Potters*, therefore, is additionally a book about the clay vessel, the essence of the ceramic tradition. By examining the clay vessels of a civilization, we may learn of its way of life as well as its art, so fundamental is their place in every society. The study of these revered objects is often inseparable from the study of religion, and numerous are the civilizations that have utilized it for religious ritual and for documentation. This becomes particularly captivating as we approach the contemporary clay vessel emerging in an environment where the public has greatest access to it: the art museum.

Although the art museum is a comparatively modern phenomenon, in many ways it is representative of the evolution of most visual art forms. Thus it may be pertinent to contrast its development with that of the vessel. It is often said that the art museum has assumed the role once held by the church as the center of cultural life. In the great European cities it was in the church that important art was commissioned, exhibited, and performed. Today these activities take place in the art museum, which testifies to the flight of all art (including the vessel) from the religious to the secular. (This movement has accelerated during the past three centuries, perhaps explaining why the United States, the secular capital of the world, has also become the capital of contemporary art.) Now it is to art museums that the masses flock in search of cultural enrichment and even spiritual enlightenment. Many museums not only exhibit art, they seek to mold the entire cultural being; thus are born "outreach programs" similar in purpose to the efforts of medieval monks, missionaries, and crusaders.

This brief analogy is particularly apt for the modern clay vessel. Like the art museum, the objects illustrated here are outgrowths of their religious predecessors, replacing religious purpose with intellectual and aesthetic concern.

As we consider the evolution of the clay vessel, its present state also suggests a metaphorical purpose. That is to say, it has become a container for ideas rather than a container for tangibles. Indeed, the "vessel as metaphor" is now an often-heard phrase in potters' studios. Painter Philip Pearlstein put this concept in focus recently when I interviewed him in New York: "Every work of art becomes metaphorical. It's an inescapable condition of being a work of art. And as a matter of fact, that's one of the criteria. When a work of art doesn't have the capability of meaning enough different things, it's dismissed as cheap entertainment." If we apply Pearlstein's criterion to our discussion, the debate over the "vessel as metaphor" is an indication that American potters are grappling with the same aesthetic issues as their counterparts in painting and sculpture.

One result of this redefinition of the vessel is a further redefinition of function. We may begin with the traditional potters: Warren MacKenzie, Karen Karnes, Kenneth Ferguson, and John Parker Glick. Adhering to the principle that pottery must have a tangible function, they fulfill this requirement without sacrificing aesthetic integrity. Utility and beauty conjoin. The subtle nuances of their work require the viewer to have an intimate rapport with the object. This is particularly true of the work of MacKenzie and Karnes.

Jerry Rothman marries form and function to a different end. Serving soup from one of his highly functional but most outrageous tureens is an experience approaching the theatrical. When not in use, Rothman's baroque forms exist as intriguing and provocative "sculptures," if you will excuse the term.

As we approach the work of Val Murat Cushing and Betty Woodman, we find function is sacrificed to the resolution of an aesthetic problem. Although one could find a use for Cushing's *Apple Jars*, clearly these oversized, extremely heavy vessels are much too cumbersome to be primarily functional. Furthermore, Cushing makes each *Apple Jar* with two distinctly different interchangeable lids, thus confronting the vessel's owner with a choice of aesthetic possibilities. Betty Woodman's pieces follow in the same suit. Although she insists her large and impressive *Pillow Pitchers* can be used, their weight and size dispute function. Clearly the primary intent here is poetry of form.

This is carried a step further with the pots and other forms of Toshiko Takaezu. These either are completely closed or have such a small opening that they are rendered nonfunctional. Vessels of this nature, as Garth Clark points out, are meant to contain space. Takaezu explores this poetic concept with her forms that encapsulate space. She translates that romantic ideal to her plates and bowls, which are very utilitarian but relate to the closed forms in feeling.

Similarly, Rudolf Staffel's small vases and bowls are created to contain or "gather" light. When light permeates the translucent porcelain bodies of his *Light Gatherers*, they come alive with subtle colors from within, while clay overlays form silhouetted patterns without.

Another level of metaphorical implementation and artistic and technical exploration is witnessed in the distinctive eclecticism of Michael Frimkess. He creates large painted china vases employing traditional Greek and Chinese shapes. At first glance these objects appear highly traditional. A closer look, however, reveals something in the spirit of "California Funk." Like Masami Teraoka and his satire on traditional Japanese woodcuts, Frimkess injects a highly historical format with his own peculiar humor. He creates an unlikely juxtaposition that reads as pure satire.

Peter Voulkos was perhaps the first ceramist to bridge the gap between painting and sculpture and ceramics. His revolutionary breakthrough of the early fifties earned a viable role for clay in the Abstract Expressionist arena. Harold Rosenberg coined the term "action painting"; Voulkos put it to work in clay. Rudy Autio also approaches vessel making in this manner, and as his recent work demonstrates, he has remained faithful to that visual vocabulary while continuing to develop new statements within its framework. His adherence to this mode is comparable to Willem de Kooning's continuing effort to produce new and fresh visions from a traditional abstract viewpoint.

Kenneth Price has also managed to work simultaneously as painter, sculptor, and ceramist. His earlier works, grounded in Futurism and Cubism, transformed the vessel into an abstract vehicle for exploring color, form, geometry, and perspective. Price then devoted five years to creating mixed-media environments in homage to Mexican folk arts, which included clay vessels as central components. These environments in a sense return the vessel to its earlier religious context, yet they are clearly Price's own creations and not merely replications of traditional forms. Price's most recent work (illustrated within) represents a return to his affinity for small, highly geometric forms. Like his earlier Cubistic oeuvre, the newer objects are based upon the format of a cup, but in a more remote fashion. Joan Simon described them in *Art in America* as "architectural models for a Futurist City or a cock-eyed aerial view of Moshe Safdie's Slab-and-Cube cluster housing."[1] Despite whatever references these pieces evoke, Kenneth Price articulates his visual vocabulary with a unique skill for infusing the small object with monumental significance.

With artists such as William Daley, Susanne Stephenson, and Richard DeVore, function is suggested but doubtful, whereas the vessel is barely recognizable in the clay paintings of Paul Soldner, where it has become a vestige, a remnant.

The contemporary vessel, like the art museum, is a modern remnant from a time when the religious and the artistic were linked. This points to the vessel's significance. Through the study of ceramics, we have gained understanding of the culture of numerous civilizations. Perhaps this can be said of most art forms, but the vessel has been our most valuable witness. It has endured time, it is universally understood, and it is one of the few art objects to cross the meaningless boundaries of art science. The vessel not only contains the real and the spiritual, but it also contains the essence of art.

Sanford Sivitz Shaman
Director, Museum of Art
Washington State University

TRANSFORMATION AND INHERITANCE

THE TRADITIONS AND AESTHETICS OF CONTEMPORARY AMERICAN CERAMICS

The artists represented in this study are among the first postwar generation of American potters. All were practicing artists or were just beginning their careers during the 1950s, the decade in which the first modern American ceramic aesthetic began to emerge after nearly two centuries of stylistic subservience to Europe.

All the artists here share the common format of the vessel; however, all consensus ends at this starting point. Indeed, the potters have been selected for their individuality in order to demonstrate the range of expression in the potter's art, from simple utility to complex symbolism.

My purpose here is to explore the route by which American potters arrived at their current state of creative and intellectual independence. This perspective, together with an examination of the aesthetic premises of the vessel through the works of the potters featured in this book, will provide the reader with a few tools with which to explore, understand, and appreciate the development of a unique contemporary pottery aesthetic in the United States.

The writer André Malraux provided a route for this journey when he noted of the creative role that "whenever artists have been great they have transfigured the forms that they inherited."[1] This is a simple but potent concept that applies to any creative medium. In this essay we will explore some of the history of the potter's "inheritance" of form and the transfiguration of this legacy through the inventive energy of the first postwar generation of American potters.

In 1950 that energy may have been apparent, but not the inventiveness. The late Bernard Leach, the noted English potter and writer, commented that the United States was without what he succinctly termed "a ceramic taproot."[2] American potters, and others working in the traditional craft mediums, were still simply imitating the forms they had inherited. This was to some extent inevitable as Americans, being mainly transplanted Europeans, did not have an indigenous cultural heritage. Therefore, the arts, including ceramics, consisted of forms borrowed and adapted from other cultures.

One could, however, charge Leach with shortsightedness, given the ground swell of cultural growth in the United States at the time. If this was not apparent in ceramics, it certainly was evident in painting, sculpture, poetry, and other arts. Barely four years after Leach's pessimistic prognostications about American ceramics, the potters of the nation were to achieve a revolution in form and content that was to produce the most vigorous realization yet of the ideal that Leach himself had established for artistic credibility—a balance between and integration of the grandeur of monistic Oriental ceramics and the demands of Western contemporary art.

Jug, England (13th–15th century), earthenware with lead glaze. Collection Metropolitan Museum of Art, New York, Rogers Fund 1924. Early English pottery was produced in strict accordance with the utilitarian needs of the community for which it was made. Despite these limitations, potters of the late medieval period produced some of the fullest and most expressive forms in English pottery.

THE WESTERN INHERITANCE: EUROPE

In order to understand this jumping-off point in modern ceramics it is pertinent to examine briefly the two primary ceramic inheritances—one from the West and the other from the East—and the manner in which these have modified our visual and conceptual approaches to the medium. We begin with the dominant influence, the development of ceramics in Europe over the past four centuries—a legacy of some ambivalence.

The handcraft purists would contest my use of the term *development*, for they see the sixteenth century as the point of decline for craftsmanship, beginning with the demise of the craft guilds and the gradual introduction of commerce and industry. William Morris, the leading voice of the English Arts and Crafts Movement, was one who held this view, noting that from this period on, Western man began for the first time to make pottery that disobeyed the "true principles" of the art's aesthetic tenets. "I should say," he declared, "that the making of ugly pottery was one of the most remarkable inventions of our civilisation."[3]

What, then, were the factors that led to the decline of Western ceramics? In the simplest terms, the decline resulted from a break between artist and craftsman

Dish by Thomas Toft, England (ca. 1680), earthenware with slip-trailed decoration under lead glaze. Collection Metropolitan Museum of Art, New York, Rogers Fund 1924. Toward the end of the medieval period growing affluence resulted in an interest in decorative wares. This demand was met by gifted potters such as Thomas Toft, until industry assumed this role in the eighteenth century.

Coffeepot by Greatbatch/Wedgwood, England (ca. 1764), lead glazes over white Devonshire clay. Collection Everson Museum of Art, Syracuse, New York. The introduction of creamware revolutionized the ceramics industry. It brought to an end the relatively inefficient tin-glaze pottery industry in Europe and, as creamware responded well to mass-production techniques, made high-quality table and decorative wares generally affordable.

and the consequent dualistic thinking that divided mind from matter in the making of ceramic objects. This is best examined by briefly tracing two technical breakthroughs that were to alter Western perceptions of ceramics: the perfection of the mass production of creamwares in England, and the discovery of the hard-paste porcelain formula on the Continent.

In English medieval society before the coming of industry, potters enjoyed a protected place in the community, serving a market of no more than twenty miles' radius. Their wares were produced with available materials and in direct response to need. The potter's lot began to change with the arrival in the 1600s of the merchant pot seller. At first the pot seller sold imported wares from Holland and Germany, but later encouraged local potters to produce decorative and functional wares.

As the pot seller marketed these goods over large distances, the potters found themselves in direct competition with one another for the first time. Those with certain advantages—proximity to good clays, water, fuel, and a large home market—prospered. But in order to survive and best make use of resources, they set up small pottery collaboratives. The "cuppers," for example, as their name suggests, made only drinking vessels to supply the huge demand resulting from the London guilds' decision to change from wooden to ceramic goblets. In this manner the corrosive practice of piecework (the undertaking of orders for large quantities of limited forms) was begun, and potters began to surrender their independence and versatility.

The affluence produced by the growth of commerce was a double-edged sword. On the one hand, it encouraged the industrial production of goods and so threatened the craftsman. On the other hand, the wealth produced in the process allowed for the production of individually decorated wares. This encouraged the potter as artist and resulted in a short but glorious period of slip decorating in England, which nurtured the genius of potters such as Thomas Toft, John Livermore, and others during the first half of the seventeenth century. The growth of industry was so rapid and all-embracing, however, that these potters were not able to secure a permanent place in the history of their country's decorative arts.

The event that revolutionized the ceramics industry was the discovery of the process of making English creamwares at the beginning of the eighteenth century and the subsequent perfection of mass-production techniques by Josiah Wedgwood. Creamwares were

Vase, Meissen, Germany (ca. 1745), hard-paste porcelain with polychrome and gold decoration. Collection The Metropolitan Museum of Art, New York, Gift of Mrs. Charles Wrightsman, 1970. The discovery of hard-paste porcelain in Europe in 1709 linked the development of "art" or fine ceramics to this new clay body. The resources required to establish a porcelain works — vast amounts of capital, aristocratic patronage, chemists and court artists — placed this medium beyond the resources of the craftsman potter and further eroded the role of the individual in European ceramics.

durable, decoratively versatile, and simple to manufacture. This invention — clear lead glaze over a white Devon clay body — sounded the death knell for the faience industry in Europe and made wares of a high quality available to the middle classes.

As industry surged ahead, riding the crest of a succession of technical improvements, the craftsman-potter was faced with the choice of making relatively crude redwares for those who could not afford the marginally higher cost of industrial whitewares, or of becoming a functionary within the factories that had sprung up around Liverpool, Leeds, Bristol, Newcastle, and Stoke-on-Trent. At first craftsmen played an important role in these early factories. The wares they produced were based upon traditional forms and were exquisitely potted and sensitively decorated.

As the market for decorative wares began to develop, Wedgwood initiated the custom of inviting fashionable painters and sculptors of the day to design

artwares. The critic Herbert Read, in a discussion of Wedgwood's role in the art-industry alliance, identified a dualism "which had never before been present in English ceramics," attributing it to Wedgwood's introduction of outside designers such as John Flaxman and Camillo Pacetti: "The source of the dualism of the 'fine' and utilitarian arts is therefore easy to trace in the limited sphere of pottery. For on the one hand we have the potter relying upon his own knowledge of the crafts and designing for use; on the other we have the artist, who is not concerned to design for use so much as for ornament — as an exhibition, that is to say, of his artistic skill and 'taste.'"[4]

It was at this point that ceramics began to lose its unity, dividing art from craft, maker from creator, functional wares from nonfunctional ones. Industry now began to ignore the craftsman's intuitive response to materials and plunged into a series of neoclassical revivals led by Wedgwood's unfortunate interest in Greek pottery. Regency restraint finally gave way to the eclectic overexuberance of the early nineteenth century. Morris noted that the potter had by now become "a convenient machine, and this machine, driven by the haphazard whims of the time, produced the most woeful set of works of art."[5]

The production of creamwares made functional and decorative wares generally accessible. The second formative innovation, the introduction of porcelain, established certain taste criteria based upon a "treasure house" concept, that rarity is more important than beauty. Revealingly, the discovery of porcelain arrived as a by-product of an attempt by alchemist Johann Böttger to produce gold from base metals for his "patron," Augustus the Strong, King of Saxony. Augustus, already an ardent collector of Chinese porcelains, established the first porcelain works in Europe at Meissen in 1709. Thereafter factories were set up under aristocratic patronage during the eighteenth century in Vienna, Nymphenburg, Sèvres, St. Petersburg, Berlin, and other centers.

Until this discovery all porcelain had come at great cost from China, and the possession of such treasures was a sign of social station — so much so that at the turn of the eighteenth century it was fashionable for the nobility to have portraits painted that showed them holding a cup and saucer or some other prized porcelain bibelot. Yet while there was a tradition of collecting porcelain prior to 1709, there was no precedent among artists and craftsmen of working in this milky, translucent clay body. At first most factories attempted to imitate Chinese originals, but gradually this chinoiserie gave over to Western styles as well, baroque and rococo.

The best use of the medium came from the sculptors who created figurines, notably Nymphenburg's Franz Anton Bustelli and Meissen's Johann Joachim Kändler, and who best exploited the liquid sensuality of the medium. For the greater part, however, there was no artistic *raison d'être* to the use of porcelain apart from being a decorative playground for the court painter and sculptor. The reason for this was that porcelain did not arrive in response to the needs of art but in order to satisfy greed.

It is a measure of the difference between Eastern and Western thinking that the Orient prized porcelain because it was one of the most beautiful of all materials, but the West valued it because it was one of the rarest of materials. The porcelain factories of Europe were looked upon as mints to create valuable objects. Whereas the porcelains of China were frequently left undecorated to exploit the pale translucency of the clay body, Western factories soon began to decorate and gild their porcelains to resemble bejeweled, golden vessels. In essence, the factories were still searching for the gold that had eluded Böttger when he stumbled on the porcelain formula.

The impact of porcelain's discovery was manifold. Now a "high" art, ceramics was beyond the reach of any individual artist or craftsman. Porcelain factories required royal patronage, vast amounts of capital, and access to the then closely guarded secrets of its manufacture and decoration.

Second, porcelain established in the West a taste for overwrought confections valued most often for the amount of ornament rather than the quality. The effect was long-lasting; even today many of us have grown up with display cabinets of porcelain trinkets and untouchable special-occasion dinnerware. These are the direct, if plebeian, descendants of the exotic *porzellankasse* that contained the porcelain treasures of the nobility at the turn of the eighteenth century. As a result, for many in the West ceramic art remains something remote and nontactile, and its only ritualistic function is to demonstrate social standing.

The 1851 Great Exhibition at the Crystal Palace in London, the first international exposition of the fruits of a nascent industrial age, dramatized the plight of the craftsman in the modern world and most particularly that of the potter. By the time of this exhibition the independent potter was almost nonexistent; the only survivors of this once vigorous craft were the so-called rustics, potters working in rural areas where the march of industrialization had not yet altered traditional life-styles. The craftsmen were replaced by corporate potters—creatures of industry—large numbers of workers with limited and highly rationalized skills organized into a production line where they threw, turned, glazed, affixed handles, and decorated according to their specialty.

It was apparent at the Great Exhibition that the potter had broken the vital thread of pedagogical tradition and continuity. Knowledge of form and material was no longer passed on from master to student, as was still the case in painting and sculpture. For the

Martin Brothers at work in their Southall studio, London. Collection Southall Library, London Borough of Ealing. The Martin Brothers were arguably the finest of the Arts and Crafts Movement potters in England. They were pioneers in establishing the identity of the artist potter as an individualistic, dedicated, self-sufficient creator.

moment, ceramics remained beyond the individual; both functional and decorative wares were now firmly captive in the impersonal machinations of industry and fashion.

Spurred on by the example of what Morris termed the Great Exhibition's "death register of design," impetus developed for that complex social, political, and aesthetic reformation that we now know as the Arts and Crafts Movement. Although a late starter, ceramics soon developed a fierce sense of mission. The ceramist sought to rebuild bridges to a rich past that industry had severed. In England many individual potters emerged in the 1870s, such as William De Morgan, who became renowned for his work in Isnik (Persian) and Hispano-Moresque glazing and decorating techniques. In common with most English ceramists, De Morgan was what Nikolaus Pevsner so accurately termed a "gentleman" potter; he was concerned with only the white-collar elements of the potter's craft and considered the handling of clay to be the province of semiskilled laborers. As a result, there was little real plastic innovation in English pottery outside the work of the gifted and prophetic Martin brothers. The English potter, however, did forge philosophical tenets for this pioneer movement and contributed a dazzling repertoire of decorating skills.

In France ceramics developed into a popular pursuit, principally under the influence of the more expressive examples of Japanese pottery. The French approach to form was more intimate and direct, and soon France developed a vanguardist role in the small but growing world of the artist-potter. By the time of the 1900 Exposition Universelle in Paris, the country could boast a cadre of masters: Ernest Chaplet; Jean

Vase by Jean Carriès, France (1889–94), stoneware with matte glaze. Collection Alain Lesieutre, Paris. Carriès, influenced by the example of Japanese ceramics, was an important figure in the artist-potter movement that grew rapidly in France from the 1870s onward. More than his contemporaries such as Ernest Chaplet and Auguste Delaherche, Carriès responded to the expressionistic license of ceramic materials. He left his throwing rings visible (even highlighting them with gold glaze) and poured, splashed, and dipped his glazes.

Vase by Vlastislav Hofman, Artel Organization, Prague (1908–14), tin-glazed earthenware. Collection Osterreichische Museum für Angewandte Kunst, Vienna. The ceramics movement in the Austro-Hungarian Empire between 1900 and 1914 showed a strong bias toward an architechtonic approach to design, in part because of the strong involvement of architects in the decorative arts who were more concerned with quality of form than with surface decoration.

Carriès, who founded a school in his style before his death in 1894; Auguste Delaherche; Pierre-Adrien Dalpayrat; Paul Jeanneney; Taxile Doat; and others. In addition, the excitement in Paris over *grand feu* (high-fired ceramics) had attracted artists from other mediums who worked intermittently in ceramics, such as Paul Gauguin, Auguste Rodin, Henri Toulouse-Lautrec, Alphonse Mucha, and Rupert Carabin. A new breed of decorative artists and industrial designers also became involved, and through Maurice Dufrene, Henri Van de Velde, Edward Colonna, and Georges de Fuere, ceramic design concepts were challenged and revolutionized.

Ceramics proved to be one of the distinguishing features of the Exposition Universelle. France's hegemony was strongly challenged by Denmark, where the artist-potter found powerful and sympathetic patrons in the form of the country's two major porcelain factories, Royal Copenhagen Porcelain and Bing and Grondahl. Finland showed the first signs of ceramic life with works by Alfred W. Finch from the Porvoo Workshop and Thure Öberg from Arabia. The United States produced an impressive showing of art pottery, with Rookwood Pottery taking the Grand Prix and several other potteries winning medals.

At this stage the approach to form was still somewhat romantic, being drawn from the past with little translation. Early in the twentieth century Austria made an impressive entrance into the field with a bold new approach to form that was geometric and constructivist in nature and aggressively modern. This interest in form was largely the result of the involvement of several progressive architects of the "form over ornament" school (Josef Hoffmann, Emile Pirchan, Joseph Maria Olbrich, Vlastislav Hofman), and so the volumetric issues of form supplanted an obsessive interest in surface, decoration, and glaze science.

By 1910 the modern ceramics movement was well under way. The three preceding decades had produced more technical innovation (new glazes, firing techniques, and decorative skills) than any other comparable period before or since. Ceramics became integrated into art schools, salons were established for its appreciation, and the first literature was produced. At that time the ceramists had successfully begun to link up with their pre-industrial past. But ahead lay an even more challenging task of bridge building that would draw ceramics into the mainstream of this century's visual arts. It is in this regard that the American potter was to play the most vital role.

Vase by Albert Valentien, Rookwood Pottery, Cincinnati, Ohio (1893), earthenware with slip painting under lead glaze. Courtesy Sotheby Parke Bernet. Rookwood Pottery was the first art pottery in the United States to win acclaim abroad. Rookwood won a gold medal at the 1889 Exposition Universelle in Paris and at the 1900 Exposition took the Grand Prix and several other honors. Although its approach to both form and decoration was highly conservative, Rookwood did serve to encourage a sense of identity and optimism in the American decorative arts movement.

Vase with stand by Adelaide Alsop Robineau, Syracuse, New York (1905), porcelain with silver blue crystalline glaze. Collection Everson Museum of Art, Syracuse. Robineau was one of the most successful studio potters in the United States. After working in the medium for a mere seven years, she received the Grand Prix for porcelain at the 1911 Turin Exposition of Decorative Art. Robineau proved that the American potter could match the formal sensitivities and skills of the European potter, but she did little to initiate a new aesthetic direction.

THE AMERICAN INHERITANCE:
THE STUDIO POTTERY MOVEMENT

In the United States art pottery got off to an early start through the energies of a group of socially prominent young women in the most unlikely Athens: Cincinnati, Ohio. Motivated by an interest in the "devil's art" of china painting around 1874, these decorators became more ambitious after the 1876 Centennial in Philadelphia. By 1878 Mary Louise McLaughlin had been able to produce a variant of the much prized *procès Barbotine* wares that she named "Cincinnati Limoges."[6] This sophisticated technique, the application of ground color with an atomizer to produce a fine gradation of tone, became the cornerstone of the art pottery movement in the United States for more than three decades.

The finest exponent of the so-called Cincinnati Faience was the Rookwood Pottery, established in 1880 by Maria Longworth Nichols. From 1883, under the shrewd management of William Watts Taylor, it became the premier American pottery; internationally known, its products were collected worldwide. Rookwood effectively developed a sense of pride and confidence in the Arts and Crafts Movement of the United States. But its market was the *petit bourgeoisie*, and so

any real innovation was frowned upon. Although the forms were clean and pleasing, little of originality was produced and the pot remained a canvas for surface decoration.

This changed at the turn of the century. William Grueby introduced art pottery to his Grueby Faience Company around 1898, and with these unpainted, monochrome-glazed wares a new aesthetic began to emerge that was based upon a more holistic interplay between strong, undecorated form, color, and texture. This grew out of the monistic aesthetic of early Chinese and Korean monochrome wares (which were now being collected and admired), from the purist structural styles in the Arts and Crafts Movement advocated by Gustav Stickley and Frank Lloyd Wright, from continental Art Nouveau, and last from the influence of the French artists-potters, particularly Delaherche, Chaplet, and Doat.

The period from 1900 onward saw the development of several strong and independent talents: Artus Van Briggle, Arthur Eugene Baggs, Adelaide Alsop Robineau, Mary Chase Perry, and George E. Ohr. With the exception of Ohr, their work reflected European stylization. The accent was undeniably American, but the language of form and decoration came from across the Atlantic Ocean. This condition was the result

Teapot by George E. Ohr, Biloxi, Mississippi (ca. 1900). Courtesy J. W. Carpenter. Ohr was the first potter to break with the stylistic dictates of Europe and develop what might be considered a native style. This potter's uniquely expressionistic sytle of handling clay, his insouciant humor, and his play with verbal and visual interchange establish him as an accurate prophet of the direction that American ceramics would take in later years.

Bowl by Maija Grotell, Bloomfield Hills, Michigan (1956), glazed stoneware. Collection Syracuse University, Syracuse, New York. Grotell was one of several Europeans who immigrated to the United States during the 1920s and 1930s and who played an important role in establishing a modern ceramics movement. Of this group Grotell emerges as the major figure, both as a teacher at the Cranbrook Academy of Art and as an artist.

partly of a self-inflicted feeling of cultural inferiority and partly of the influence of the many Europeans who worked in ceramics in the United States during the early twentieth century.

The dominant educational institution in American ceramics, the New York State College of Clayworking and Ceramics at Alfred University, was directed from its inception in 1900 by Charles Fergus Binns, son of the director of the Royal Worcester porcelain works in England. The erudite Frederick Hurten Rhead, also from England, established himself as one of the major designers and spokespersons for the field. From France came Taxile Doat, then at the height of his fame, to teach at the Ceramic Art Institute of the People's University, University City, St. Louis. Jacques Sicard, a disciple of France's Clement Massier, worked with Weller Pottery for some time, producing distinctive if overripe "Sicardowares" with an iridescent glaze.

One potter remained aloof from the seductive styles of Europe: George E. Ohr, the self-styled "new Palissy." Ohr worked in Biloxi, Mississippi, from the 1880s and was noted for his bizarre behavior, his long trailing mustache, and his skill at the wheel. Until recently, however, he was looked upon as a southern curiosity rather than an artist of consequence. In 1972 the chance discovery of a hoard of more than six thousand of his pieces in the Ohr family warehouse (including most of the major works made during the last ten to fifteen years of his career) altered this paternalistic view of a man who must now be acknowledged as the first American artist-potter, both chronologically and stylistically.

Ohr's distinctive style of working was to throw paper-thin forms that he would then ruffle, pummel, twist, and, as Robert Blasberg so evocatively puts it, "wring the necks of."[7] The overall effect of this shaping, combined with some of the most expressionistic surface treatment of the day, was furious urgency and gesture. The choice of deliberately anthropomorphic form gave a sensual, often erotic overtone to much of the work. Ohr also indulged a taste for verbal and visual references, producing top hats, pornographic buttons, and money banks that playfully meddle with language, form, and taste in the same way Funk artists would some sixty years later.

Ohr decided to withdraw from the marketplace at the turn of the century and hoard his serious pieces. As a result, his work was rapidly forgotten until its dramatic reappearance in 1972. One cannot therefore claim that Ohr was an influence until quite recently; however, that does not in any way diminish the uncanny accuracy and clarity of his prophecy. In Ohr's work are the foundations of an unfettered play with form and material that was to distinguish the most avant-garde expression of the post–World War II ceramist.

Between the two world wars the European presence in the United States increased rather than diminished. The 1925 Exposition in Paris drew considerable attention, and Adelaide Robineau, the editor of *Keramik Studio*, wrote a series of ten articles that brought the achievements of the Scandinavians, Austrians, French, and English to the attention of American potters.[8] Several major ceramists moved from Europe to the United States: Maija Grotell from Finland; Vally Wieselthier, Susi Singer, and Gertrud and Otto Natzler from Austria; the French-born Bauhausler Marguerite Wildenhain and her German husband, Frans; Paul Bonifas from Switzerland; and briefly, from England, the surrealist Sam Haile. All proved to be strong influences through the 1950s.

This Art Deco—Art Moderne period was a time of mixed achievement. For the ceramic sculptor it proved to be a progressive era, introducing as it did a figurative genre that employed a bright polychrome palette and a rowdy, insouciant sense of humor that continues to be characteristic of American ceramics. The potter's achievement was uneven, however. Some fine work was produced, but either fully within a European aesthetic or at least with frequent glances over the shoulder for a nod of approval from across the Atlantic. Alfred University was partly the root of this condition, as it continued to expound an academic, design-based approach to the ceramic aesthetic through the 1930s until the arrival of Charles Harder.

Glen Lukens pinpointed the impasse that this presented when he wrote in 1937 of the lifeless quality of a pot arrived at by a process of conscious design. Design, he asserted, led most frequently to cleverness rather than originality, and a spiritual concern was necessary that would replace stylistic invention with a greater sensitivity to process and thereby self-discovery. This was an important statement, coming as it did several years before Leach's writings in the same vein.[9]

The two decades were not wasted for the potter, proving to be a necessary watershed. American potters were able to satisfy themselves that they could match the craftsmanship of Europeans and that the mysteries of the craft per se were not as profound as they had once thought.

Art critics were beginning to sense the latent energy in ceramics. In 1937 the art editor of *Fortune* magazine wrote that "against the broad perspective of ancient excellence the work of the American ceramists has been artistically infinitesimal. . . . it has its admirers of the days of the early Colonial potters to those of the late gifted Adelaide Robineau but in comparison with Europe and the East, it has lacked even the high point from which to decline." The writer continued, referring to works from the Syracuse Museum of Fine Art's Ceramic National Exhibition, which was then on view at the Whitney Museum in New York, that this

Untitled plate by Peter Voulkos, Berkeley, California (1963), stoneware, thrown and torn. Courtesy Quay Gallery, San Francisco. Peter Voulkos and the group that grew around him, first at the Los Angeles County Art Institute and then at the University of California in Berkeley, produced a progressive, questioning, and at times anarchistic spirit in ceramics that, through the fifties and sixties, transformed the pottery aesthetic in the United States.

exhibition was "of more than fashionable interest. . . . American ceramic art is beginning to show signs of life."[10]

The breakthrough came in the mid-1950s with a group of students who gathered around Peter Voulkos at the Los Angeles County Art Institute (now the Otis/Parsons Art Institute) between 1954 and 1957. This flash point has been well documented, so it is unnecessary to do more than outline some of the artistic freedoms gained by this collaborative experiment. The students and teachers (and these roles were not fixed) pursued Harold Rosenberg's ideal of art as an unfocused play with materials. In keeping with the existentialist view of humanity then prevalent, Rosenberg argued that artists who practiced "action painting" (his term) were exercising their "authentic being" through acts of creation. The finished works were only a record of their being. Likewise, there was no commitment to craftsmanship per se by Voulkos and his students. As Paul Soldner, the first of the Otis students, recalls, there was no pressure to produce exhibitable work.

Nonetheless, the production of the group was awesome. Some weeks saw hundreds of pots being slabbed, thrown, assembled, painted, pummeled, and torn. Most were discarded by the artists or destroyed by the kiln. The energies at Otis came from the new American confidence that the success of Abstract Expressionism had generated in the visual arts, as well as from jazz and Beat poetry. Europe continued to play a role, and perhaps the strongest early influence on Voulkos was the pottery of Pablo Picasso, Joan Miró, and other European artists then working in clay.

The principal format of the group was the vessel, and the wheel remained their major tool and source of formal energy. It was not until the Otis experiment came to an end in 1957 and Voulkos moved to the University of California at Berkeley (1958) that sculptural, nonvessel concerns were explored in any depth. By this stage a group had grown loosely around Voulkos that included Paul Soldner, Billy Al Bengston, John Mason, Jerry Rothman, Michael Frimkess, Henry Takemoto, and Malcolm McClain. Soon after Voulkos's arrival in Berkeley, Jim Melchert, Ron Nagle, and others joined this pottery revolution.

Not until 1961 was the art world at large introduced to this "new ceramic presence," as Rose Slivka characterized the development in her article published that year in *Craft Horizons*.[11] The West Coast art community was of course no stranger to Voulkos and company. Critic and painter Peter Plagens, in his book *Sunshine Muse* (1974), singled out this group as one of the most important influences on California painting and one that was instrumental in the development of polychrome metal sculpture in the early sixties. The craft movement, however, of which the Otis group was still a member by virtue of an archaic and inflexible material apartheid, was scandalized. The American Crafts Council, publisher of *Craft Horizons*, was inundated with letters of protest and cancellations of membership as a result of Slivka's article.

The outrage stemmed from the fact that the work of the Voulkos group represented the antithesis of the Western pottery aesthetic. The conservative canons of the ceramics community were under attack. The pottery that was illustrated ignored the West's obsession with carefully balanced neoclassical form and instead was assertively asymmetrical. The clay was used with some violence, and surfaces were painted, slashed, and torn in a manner that challenged the three-dimensional form, rather than complemented it, which was the Western tradition.

The new form language had a precedent in the more radical expressions of Zen beauty in Japanese pottery. The potters in the West were of course familiar with the Oriental and particularly the Japanese traditions. But through the modern movement potters had taken from the East only what reinforced classical Western modes of expression. There were exceptions, such as France's Jean Carriès and England's William Staite Murray, but generally this holds true. What Voulkos had found in Japanese aristocratic wares (not folkwares, as is usually suggested) was the means with which to transfigure the Western inheritance.

Although the ceramics community at first found this work to be a threat to its concept of "good taste" (an important criterion at the time), they soon warmed to the provocative inventions of the Otis group. Within the group itself and farther afield in the rest of the country, the new freedom of expression was interpreted by each artist in his or her own manner. Those at Otis cannot claim to have established a new style as such, but they did expand the parameters of the pottery aesthetic and in so doing placed American ceramics on the map for the first time.

THE MODIFYING INHERITANCE: JAPAN

Before proceeding with a discussion of the contemporary pot, let us first briefly examine the synergism that developed between Western and Japanese pottery, what was drawn from these traditions, and how the cultural bridging took place. It is undoubtedly Bernard Leach who must be given the credit for laying the foundation for this interchange. He possessed an intimate understanding and experience of the East. In his pottery he was unable to lose a certain academicism in his play between East and West; however, Leach assumed a major role as propagandist, awakening the Western potter to a Zen aesthetic that grew out of life and not out of design. Leach was one of several artists, scholars, and intellectuals who assembled at Dartington Hall, a progressive school in England, during the 1930s. The group included his close friend Mark Tobey, Ravi Shankar, Pearl Buck, and Aldous Huxley. All shared an interest in the Orient, and particularly in Zen concepts of beauty, and saw therein the seeds for a revitalization of Western art.

Leach's first visit to the United States came in 1950, when he was already something of a legend. He had published *A Potter's Book* in 1940, which was immediately adopted as the bible of the studio potter. By association Leach became the messiah, a role he accepted most willingly. During his visit he received the Binns Medal of the American Ceramic Society. Two years later he returned with the Japanese potter Shoji Hamada and Soetsu Yanagi, the philosopher and founder of the Japanese folk art movement. The trio lectured throughout the United States, drawing large audiences and meeting many of the artists who were later to provide leadership in the field: Peter Voulkos, Rudy Autio, Karen Karnes, Robert Turner, and others.

Through Leach, American potters learned of the Orient in a new sense. The Oriental aesthetic is that beauty derives not from the victory of science or craft but from the sensitivity of every element of the process by which an object has been made. A pot is therefore a diary of a journey, and this is the root of its aesthetic worth, not the conscious striving for intellectually held visual principles. In one of his best writings, "Belief and Hope," Leach set out this credo:

In our day the threads have been loosened and a creative mind finds itself alone with the responsibility of discovering its own meaning and pattern out of all traditions and all cultures. Without achieving integration or wholeness he cannot encompass the extended vision and extract from it a true synthesis. The quality

Bottle by Bernard Leach, St. Ives, England (ca. 1960), Tenmoku glazed stoneware. Collection Syracuse University, Syracuse, New York. In the United States, Leach encouraged the bridging of Eastern and Western poles of thought. Those who drew from the philosophical tenets expressed by Leach found his sense of mission to be invigorating and timely. In the United States as in England, however, a "Leach school" developed that simply imitated the works of Leach and of the classical periods in China, Korea, and Japan without any attempt to infuse a contemporary intelligence and interpretation. The dogmatic approach of these "monkey-see, monkey-do" traditionalists unfortunately contributed to the backlash against the vessel and traditionalist values that occured during the 1960s.

Pitcher by Shoji Hamada, Japan (ca. 1966), salt-glazed stoneware with slips. Collection University of Michigan Art Museum, Ann Arbor. This work represents an interesting cultural confluence. Its character is undeniably Japanese, but the handle and the salt-glazed surfaces are Western innovations that have been explored in Japanese ceramics only during this century.

which appears to me fundamental in all pots is life in one or more of its modes: inner harmony, nobility, purity, strength, breadth and generosity, or even exquisiteness and charm. But it is one thing to make a list of virtues in man and pot and another to interpret them in the counterpoint of convex and concave, hard and soft, growth and rest, for this is the breathing of the Universal in the particular.[12]

What was further intriguing about the Japanese tradition was the early celebration of ceramic artists, their individualism and independence. This was new to the West. With the exception of few artists such as the Della Robbia family in Renaissance Italy and the French Mannerist Bernard Palissy, the concept of a self-sufficient ceramic artist had not been promoted in the West until the late nineteenth century. In Japan the artist-potter had emerged three centuries earlier, and early masters such as Chojiro, Koetsu, Ninsei, and Kenzan acquired the status of artists in their society.

This early appreciation of ceramic art grew into a highly sophisticated pursuit through the tea ceremony (*cha-no-yu*), a meditative ritual that evolved under a series of tea masters into a form of religious aestheticism encompassing all the utensils and the environment of the ceremony. The ceremony spread from the aristocracy to the middle class, creating a market for tea bowls and other utensils. Master potters found active encouragement of their art, and the tradition of making tea bowls and other ceramic vessels has continued uninterrupted through the twentieth century. Today the best traditional potters in Japan are honored with the title of National Living Treasure and are revered by their society.

What intrigued the Western potter about the Japanese tradition was the importance placed upon the sensual, tactile qualities of the medium. In the West ceramic appreciation was through the eye and the mind alone. This is understandable, given the fact that the most prized ceramic objects in the West were not created by potters. Therefore, forms developed that seemed attractive on the drawing board but in practice were poorly suited to their function and material, denying the objects the more generous and common qualities of clay. The visually elegant Empire-style teacups with their awkward curvilinear handles are a good case in point.

The handle itself, unknown until the twentieth century in Japanese ceramics, was another alienating element of Western tradition in that it separates the user from direct contact with the main form. In Japan, by contrast, the cupping of the tea bowl in the hands is one of the primary aesthetic pleasures of the tea ceremony and a means of determining true form. Generally, eating in Japan involves direct handling of the pottery. In the West the knife and fork separate one from the plate; indeed, until recently the plate was not handled at all in better middle-class homes but was placed on the table and removed by servants.

Most decorative ceramic objects, those "untouchables" of the display cabinet, were conceived with the same lack of interest in tactile qualities, a fact that discouraged any intimacy with delicate china painting and encrustations of relief ornament. This all conspired to bring about a condition in the West that Philip Rawson pungently describes as a "sensuous castration."[13]

The desire to restore tactilism as a quality of modern ceramics drew many potters to Japanese ceramics. This extended beyond simply appreciating pleasant surfaces, however. Although Japanese pottery tends to be intensely cerebral—even the rough Bizen and Shigaraki wares with their carefully cultivated "chance" defects—the works exhibited an appealing physicality that the West had not enjoyed for several centuries. The potter Kanjiro Kawai highlighted this difference of perception when asked how he identified good pottery. "With my body," he replied.[14]

Bottle by Kanjiro Kawai, Japan (ca. 1955), glazed stoneware. Private collection. The Japanese artist potters played an important role during the turbulent years of change in American ceramics. Staunchly independent figures such as Kawai, Hamada, Rosanjin, and others provided an example and model for the American potter to emulate. Moreover, they were able to communicate an aesthetic response to the pottery that was philosophically different from that of the West, based as it was upon a monistic Zen Buddhist view of creativity.

This combination of cerebral and intuitive physical perception became more understandable to the Western potter when Abstract Expressionist painting provided a viewpoint from which traditional Japanese pottery could find a contemporary context. Potters discovered that the furious energy that began to cover American canvases in the 1940s and 1950s had parallels in Japanese pottery that extended back for centuries: the nonrepresentative use of color, the abstract play with materials, poured and splashed pigments, asymmetrical form and composition, the exploitation of happenstance—in short, both were art forms of gesture and risk.

The combination of these two influences, one from pottery's past and the other from painting's present, provided just the chemistry needed to create a new and exploratory form language. If one summarized the influence of Japanese pottery in particular and Zen aestheticism in general, it could be said that this engendered in the American potter a new self-confidence expressed through both body and mind. As Voulkos explains, "The clay moves; one must learn to dance with it." As a result, potters now established a vigorous new expressiveness tied both to their singular past and to current concerns in the contemporary arts. The dance had begun.

THE VESSEL AS AESTHETIC PREMISE

Pottery has grown conceptually over the past three decades, but it has been decidedly slow in gaining a critical audience in the fine-arts community. This condition is the result of what John Coplans terms the "hierarchy of materials" as well as the myopic attitudes within ceramics itself. After the initial burst of energy at Otis, many from the Otis group and later at the University of California at Berkeley turned away from the vessel and toward ceramic sculpture. According to Coplans, members of the Otis group had "suffered anguish" because their work was still consigned to the twilight world of craft and not seriously appreciated alongside the other arts.

Early in the 1960s it became apparent that certain terms, notably *pot* and *potter*, had become unacceptable in art circles. Increasingly one saw statements about artists having "turned pottery into sculpture and craft into art." An antipottery faction developed in the universities that denounced making vessels and favored making sculptural objects.

Some potters responded by making grotesquely androgynous objects that potter Wayne Higby has delightfully labeled "sculpt-a-pots," pots that impersonate sculpture. With few exceptions the term can be used as a euphemism for both poor pottery and poor sculpture. It was common practice, however, to talk of a mediocre pot as pottery and an exceptional pot as sculpture. This was a sad attempt to confer re-

spectability through association with the higher arts. Few artists, or critics for that matter, sought to ally the vessel with its own proud six-thousand-year history.

Poor scholarship in critically examining pottery, reinforced by the incestuous self-help tendencies of the pottery community itself, which discouraged independent critics, contributed to this malaise of identity. Both Slivka and Coplans, two of the most independent critics involved in the early years of the postwar clay movement, had the regrettable tendency to write of ceramics as a subcategory of either painting or sculpture.

A more current example of this contrariness can be found in the introduction to the catalog *West Coast Ceramics* by the director of Amsterdam's Stedelijk Museum, Edy de Wilde. Speaking of Voulkos's pots, he admits that they do "look like" huge pots, but concludes finally that they are not, "because their sole purpose appeared to be the visualization of volume and form, sculpture in other words."[15]

Quite the contrary is true, in fact; pottery has always been concerned with the visualization of volume and form, and this remains the central focus of the potter today—unlike sculpture, which has largely rejected volumetric form as being nineteenth-century in conception. Herbert Read notes that pottery has always been more free to express the abstract "will to form" than other visual mediums, as it has traditionally been free of imitative intent—a freedom that sculpture has only recently been able to grasp.[16]

Even those institutions to which the potter looks for reinforcement appear insensitive to the depth of the art. The American Craft Council ran an advertisement in *Craft Horizons* for the book *Peter Voulkos: A Dialogue with Clay* in which the following claim was made: "For thousands of years a pot was simply a hollow or spherical form, usually handbuilt and fired . . . until Peter Voulkos came along." Apart from the indirect suggestion that throwing was a California innovation, this summary dismissal of millennia of achievement indicates the poor understanding of this medium's past.

This situation is painful to the serious potter and has been responsible for the isolationist stance that has identified the field for so long. The positive consequence, however, was to cause many potters to redouble their efforts to achieve understanding and win a place in the nation's arts community. The creation in the past decade of several new galleries that are particularly supportive of the vessel aesthetic—Helen Drutt Gallery in Philadelphia; Exhibit A in Chicago; Yaw Gallery in Birmingham, Michigan; and Okun-Thomas Gallery in St. Louis—has assisted in addressing the problem of aesthetic credibility by building the nucleus for a discerning audience.

The art critics have welcomed the return of pottery to categorical clarity. The following comment by Kenneth W. Jones in the *Philadelphia Arts Exchange* is of particular interest. His remarks were part of a review of the one-person exhibition by Richard DeVore (a long-standing and unrepentant pottery chauvinist) at the Helen Drutt Gallery:

> Convulsing from the perplexities of his or her placement in the hierarchy of art, the ceramist has often rejected both the utilitarian aspect of pottery as well as its history as an art. Denying a chain of events can in itself be useful and even produce a new event, but too often repeated it becomes dogma based on a false or nonexistent foundation. As a solution to the problem many ceramists view their art as a sort of mini-sculpture; in consciously rejecting their own discipline, however, they frequently fail to realize that they have attached themselves to another. The resultant breakdown in communication creates bewilderment in the audience and frustration in the artist.[17]

Jones saw viability in DeVore's hard-line insistence that his work be addressed as pottery and not sculpture, noting that some healthy soul searching was now taking place in many areas of art's collective past; historians and practitioners alike were evaluating points of departure that helped to create the present state of the arts. Historian Philip Rawson agrees with the notion of a change being in the offing for the potter:

> Another revolution in art may well demand that work be addressed to the whole multi-sensuous man, hands and all, to awaken those important and intensely valuable regions of feeling and sensual order which pure visual-abstract work ignores, or even affronts. In this revolution a complete re-evaluation of the meaning of ceramics could play as vital a part as did the rediscovery of African sculpture in an earlier revolution. And there is no reason at all why lines of thought taking up from one or another of humanity's past ceramic achievements should not be picked up again, and developed along radical new lines.[18]

The revived interest in pottery is evidenced in many ways. The Philadelphia, St. Louis, and Denver museums of art now prominently exhibit pottery in their permanent displays of contemporary American art. For the first time Sotheby's is auctioning pottery by living artists in its august Belgravia salesrooms. Potters are enjoying this change in status, both because of their energetic achievements of the past three decades and because of a general move back toward decorative art, toward intimacy and the expressive touch of the maker's hand.

George Woodman, a professor of art at the University of Colorado at Boulder, dealt with this issue in an address delivered at the Ceramics Symposium: 1979 in Syracuse, New York:

> There has recently emerged an articulate group of artists who reject a great deal of recent avant garde art as elitist, sexist, racist and capitalistic, and who find the whole possibility of decoration exhilarating and broadening. I tend to be very sympathetic with these artists and find that much of the art which we have seen in the last 15 years is drab and boring. There is an

influential and subversive movement in American art today ready to reconsider the whole relationship of decorative art and so-called fine or serious art. The future we hope for ceramics may not consist in finally bubbling up through the aesthetic soup to the top little bit of scum where the "fine" arts are, but in fact the whole thing may be about to turn over.[19]

FUNCTION AS AN AESTHETIC PREMISE

For the Westerner the difficulty in appreciating pottery often stems from its association with function. In essence this is inescapable, for all pottery form as we know it today evolved out of utilitarian roots. Closed forms, such as bottles and lidded jars, were developed for the storage of food; open forms—plates and bowls—for serving. Functionalism, therefore, is the mother of pottery form. What differs from potter to potter is what Rawson sees as "symbolic projection": employing the artistic metaphor of the pot to create a relationship with the viewer that deals with intellectual and visual content rather than utilitarianism. Although symbolic projection might give the pot conceptual rather than utilitarian function, however, this does not imply that the aesthetic worth of a utilitarian piece is any less. Leach explained that for the functional potter, the discipline needed to achieve a certain level of beauty is every bit as rigorous as that of the maker of the art pot:

> A potter on his wheel is doing two things at the same time: he is making hollow wares to stand upon a level surface for the common usage of the home, and he is exploring space. His endeavour is determined in one respect by use, but in other ways by a never-ending search for perfection of form. Between the subtle opposition and interplay of centrifugal and gravitational force, between straight and curve (ultimately of sphere and cylinder, the hints of which can be seen between the foot and lip of every pot), are hidden all the potter's experience of beauty. Under his hands the clay responds to emotion and thought from a long past, to his own intuition of the lovely and the true, accurately recording the stages of his own inward development. The pot is the man; his virtues and his vices are shown therein—no disguise is possible. The virtues of the pot are derived from the familiar virtues of life.[20]

Our apparent unease with function in art is understandable. With few exceptions—Roger Fry's attempt to find functional expression for his art through his Omega Workshop pottery, the Dadaists' anarchistic "art into life" crusade, Vladimir Tatlin's concept of the "artist-engineer" as the servant of the proletariat—modern culture is identified by a sharp division between art and function. Art is something encountered in imposing marble museums rather than in the home.

Again, comparison with Japanese values becomes relevant. The Japanese, through the tea ceremony and an all-pervading domestic aestheticism, did not see art in the West's dualistic terms. To them, art and life were one, and the achievement of this monistic goal was one of life's great mysteries and challenges.

Scandinavia provides the only European example comparable to Japan; the harsh climate forces long periods indoors, encouraging what historian Alf Gard af Segerstad terms "domestic culture," the cultivation of an artistic living milieu, that is a major focus in these northern countries. This resulted in creative talent being channeled toward design rather than the fine arts and was responsible for Scandinavia's energetic entry into, and domination of, modern design in the 1950s.

For the greater part, Western rituals did not result in the same unity of art and life. Instead, the schism between the two has grown wider. This difference in our cultural response is caused by many factors, predominantly the speed with which industry and the resultant commercialization overtook our lives. In response to the growth of bourgeois materialism in our society, artists began to adopt an idealistic socialist stance that considered objects and their connoisseurship to be unsupportably decadent and middle-class.

For a short period in the 1920s and 1930s, when the cultish "Machine Art" attitudes were being promulgated by the Museum of Modern Art in New York and the Royal Academy of Art in London, it seemed as though a marriage between art and industry was again in the offing. A fashionable interest in communism within the artistic community led artists to consider making their work available to the proletariat. Michael Cardew, while running a country workshop pottery in the 1930s, recalls that he finally succumbed to peer pressure to attempt to apply his knowledge to the greater good—that is, design for industry.

For Cardew, and for most of those who attempted to bring about the idealistic union, the marriage was never properly consummated. The parties were temperamentally and ideologically incompatible from the outset. Many of the artists approached this challenge in a dilettante manner, however, and at heart had little real interest in making their work available to the masses. During the Art Deco period, however, artists produced some of the best industrial ceramics to be seen. The efforts of Kasimir Malevich, Nikolai Suetin, and Ilia Chashnik in producing Suprematist ceramics for the Leningrad State Porcelain Factory; Frank Brangwyn's designs for Royal Doulton Pottery; and Paul Nash's and John Armstrong's designs for Wilkinson Pottery are notable examples.

This "Machine Art" vogue began to wane in the mid-1930s and did not resurface after the Second World War. Instead, the role of the artist became increasingly esoteric. The Abstract Expressionists, Minimalists, and Conceptualists regarded craftsmanship as a Victorian concept.

The vanguardist notion was to reject conventional objecthood and its attendant reverence for skills, substituting the goal of creating an aesthetic experi-

Double-spouted coffeepot by Theo Bogler, Bauhaus Pottery Workshop, Dornburg aan de Salle, Germany (ca. 1924), earthenware. Courtesy National Museum, Stockholm. The Functionalist creed of the Bauhaus had an ambivalent influence upon Western ceramics. In some ways it encouraged a less dogmatic, less romantic approach to form and function, in other ways the Bauhaus resulted in a somewhat puritanical approach to function, devoid of humor, ritual, symbolism, and ornament.

ence. Occasionally this approach did result in a more or less formal object, such as a painting or a temporary sculptural form; however, transient and impermanent mediums predominated, leading to a succession of environmental, performance, and process modes of expression. The purpose of such art was to stress being, not making.

This direction in Western art seems to be currently becalmed. It continues as one of many genres but no longer rules as the unquestioned high priest of art. Its decline has been the result of new focuses developing in the arts, a more conservative climate overall, and the spuriousness of some conceptual art theory. As the potter reveals more clearly than most, making does not negate being. Indeed, the potter has sought for the greater part of modern history to deny this dualism that so pompously divides mind from matter.

Nonetheless, art has emerged in the eighties with an inordinate ambivalence toward functionalism. Thus the makers of utilitarian pottery, who also aspire to the role of artists, have the greatest difficulty achieving credibility in art terms. At the same time they are among our most valuable artists, keeping intact the thin, vulnerable bridge that enables us to experience beauty through use.

Function is in addition a loaded term, as is most of the terminology defining the semantic mine field dividing art from craft. Our difficulty stems from seeing functionalism as synonymous with design. Design, in turn—and in particular good design—has been canonized within the *neue sachlichkeit* ("new objectivity") principles of the modernist movement, led by the German Bauhaus. The Bauhaus created an ideological base for design and introduced the capital *F* to functionalism. This view proved to be a moralistic, political notion of function, which strove to embody those qualities thought to be for the greater good. What resulted was a commendable if sterile list of qualities: moderate price, simple unadorned form, efficiency, and hygiene. Good design represented the ordered vision of a perfect socialist society.

These values were best assumed by industry, which was structured to deal with the rigid standardization that this view of design requires. The role of functional potters in our age must be different. For if they are to take on principles that have been created expressly for an industrial age, the relatively inefficient potters will be outpaced from the outset. Instead, they are free to go in search of the mysteries of expression that industry, governed by the inexorable process of rationalization, must exclude.

There are some important questions that must be asked: Do we, in the post-industrial age, really want good design as the modernist movement has defined it? Have our needs altered in this decade? What do we now expect from functionalism? Good function can be simply defined as satisfaction of a need. For many of us the need is not for absolute efficiency. For instance, eating and drinking provide a potential source of ritual in our daily lives. It is in this area of psychological need that we look to the potter for utensils to enliven our daily lives through art. After all, what enables us to use industrially made pottery with such indifference is the undemanding nature of efficient design. Efficiency as an ideal in itself treads a narrow line between practicality and boredom.

In examining some of the utilitarian vessels in this book there are many objects that, although they are intended to function (for instance, Jerry Rothman's fleshy soup tureens), appear to be textbook examples of poor design. Rothman's baroque vessels do serve the role of tureens most effectively, but the artist has had the greatest difficulty convincing his collectors of this fact, repeatedly being told that they are "visual," not functional. In fact, the only hindrance in appreciating them in utilitarian terms is our baggage of preconceived notions as to what is and is not a functional soup tureen.

Teacup by Betty Woodman, Boulder, Colorado (1978), glazed stoneware. Private collection. An identifying characteristic of American ceramics is the *laissez-faire* approach to function. The search for effective form overcomes textbook considerations regarding utility. This teacup, for instance, has too small a base and too wide a mouth, yet it "functions" so well in an aesthetic sense that one is prepared to make the effort to overcome its shortcomings in terms of efficiency.

This distinction between good design and good function needs to be explored a little further. Perhaps the best explanation is a brief personal anecdote. A couple of years ago when Betty Woodman was teaching at Scripps College in southern California, we held impassioned debates, into the early hours of the morning, about function and in particular what I saw as the "poor" design of her cups. The feet were small and totally overbalanced by the tuliplike form that surmounted them. This shape was so open that coffee or tea cooled within minutes of being poured. In conventional terms they were badly designed. Nonetheless, I accepted a gift of these cups and after a while learned a lesson about function.

As a compulsive coffee drinker I had always used the classic "diner" coffee mug. It was stable and allowed me to take sips of coffee while working without concern about the mug's overbalancing. Coffee drinking became an unconscious activity; as a result, I rarely tasted the beverage and frequently it was forgotten, left to grow cold and undrinkable. Attracted by the aesthetic appeal of Betty's cups, I began to use them. After a while it became apparent that they had surreptitiously enforced a ritual. To avoid spilling coffee in these precarious cups, I was obliged to leave my work and sit quietly for a while to concentrate on drinking. Several times each day I would become engrossed and refreshed by this simple but pleasing ceremony. It became apparent that "good" design, in the moralistic sense, has little relationship to the broader sphere of human needs. The term *function* must ultimately find personal definition.

Coffeepots by Michael Cardew, Abuja, Nigeria. Glazed stoneware. Private collection. Cardew has played a major role in developing a functionalist spirit among the Western potters, based more upon a Western root of classicism than upon Oriental mysticism. In this sense he is not a part of the "Leach school," as is so often stated, but has offered an alternative to Leach's philosophical approach.

The adherence of the potter to traditional forms that we identify as functional (whether they are utilitarian or not) provides a starting point, a given premise, for form exploration—much the same situation (albeit with more dynamic variables) as the painter accepting the canvas as format. Even Voulkos, one of the most radical potters, retains the identifiable forms of plate and pot. When asked why he did not instead adopt forms more related to his metal sculpture, he replied, "I make plate and pot forms because when I am working with clay, these are the forms that I can relate to."[21]

This blunt statement pinpoints the nub of the issue. The concept of function, regardless of how distant it may become through "symbolic projection," remains the most powerful metaphor of all because it is one we can *all* relate to. From this root are derived the abstract polarities of pottery form: at one end the containment of space; at the other, the serving of space.

It is from Michael Cardew that we take the last word on function. We might acknowledge its existence, but we do not have to employ it as a divisive concept. All the work in this book "functions" in some manner or other, even if the function is to provide decorative pleasure. Cardew warns that we should not become victims of dualistic thinking that "either you make utility ware or else you are a ceramic artist making things not meant for use at all." In response to the question "Why make functional pottery in the twentieth century?" Cardew wrote:

The true successors of those old craftsmen are the modern potters who now, in the happier and more relaxed context of today, are making the same response to form, not primarily from an economic or commercial motive but chiefly because "absolute form" inspires them to work in the same way. They are liberated from the dualistic habit of thinking. Like the village potters of West Africa they see no difference between their own work—creating living forms for daily use—and that of the free ceramic sculptor, who makes forms for nonutilitarian purposes.[22]

THE VESSEL: AESTHETIC DYNAMICS

Cardew's argument carries on into the discussion of the aesthetic quality of pottery:

All our anxious discussions and argumentations about function and functionalism, about the changing needs of different periods or generations—all those questions like: "Is it valid to make functional pots in the age of Continuous Technological Revolution?" "What is the purpose or *raison d'être* of ceramic creation?" "Should we be making utensils, or producing ceramic fantasies?" All these debates are unnecessary, wasting our time and the time of our friends and contemporaries. Pottery is about one thing only: *the majesty of form*.[23]

What then is the source of this majesty? Cardew sees this in the broadest sense: a response to the universe as we perceive it—"the shape in which we live." It is necessary, however, to narrow this view somewhat to establish what differentiates pottery form from form in other mediums.

The key to understanding pottery form is that pottery is an art of limitations. Its form has changed little in six thousand years, even in the hands of its more radical exponents: Voulkos, Rudi Staffel, and Jerry Rothman. The elements of foot, belly, shoulder, neck, mouth, and lip remain constant. The challenge of the art is to find unique expression within these limitations.

Leach has argued that when potters make a vessel, they are exploring space. In essence this is true. But the same could be said of filmmakers, painters, or sculptors, all of whom have greater freedom to explore space than potters. The potter's limitation is being restricted to dealing with form through the *enclosure* of space. It is the distribution of the spatial volume that is the primary source of aesthetic power: swelling, thrusting, enfolding, closing, opening. While potters are dealing with volume, so too are they dealing with mass, the *displacement* of space. The interplay between these two forces—inner-outer, positive-negative—provides the crucial visual energy in the vessel's aesthetic.

Where the tension between inner and outer form is finely tempered, a quality develops that for lack of a better term I refer to as *resonance*. This is essentially what one means when speaking of a pot's having presence, seeming to occupy a greater space than it physically displaces. The key to this resonance is in the thin thrown, hand-built, or cast wall of the vessel that divides the inner and outer space. When a pot is created with sensitivity, these walls become pulsating membranes recording the subtleties of interplay between containment and displacement.

Although all pottery can be said to deal with inner and outer space, certain artists stress this element and consciously make it a central visual focus: DeVore with the relationship between his carefully drawn rims and pierced walls; Voulkos through his puncturing and slashing of plate and vessel walls; Turner through impressing marks and shapes deep into the plastic surface of his pots; Woodman with her incised baskets. Bill Daley's works, however, are almost entirely about positive and negative form. The architectonic stepped and terraced structures constantly draw the eye backward and forward between the implications and juxtapositions of negative and positive form.

Line plays a vital role in formally analyzing a pottery form. The dominant linear element is perhaps the outer, defining profile. This profile provides us with the shape of the vessel while suggesting movement of line and extended space. Essentially there are three main profiles in pottery, each with a specific implication regarding volume. The first, and a profile most common in the West, is best illustrated in the work of Val Cushing.

In Cushing's lidded jars and casseroles the profile follows the edge of the form and then turns back into the vessel. The line of the lid does much the same thing. This has the effect of creating an overpowering, womblike sense of containment that implies two inner volumes, one male and the other female. In such work—and Toshiko Takaezu's bottle forms have a similar finite sense of containment—the volumetric statement is so dominant that the resonance between inner and outer space becomes more static, if no less electric.

The second profile deals with a different projection of line and volume, suggesting a continuity of the pot's space beyond the object itself. An English art theorist has given this the grotesquely imperialistic title of "colonized space." I prefer to use the term *implied space*, as its existence is defined by linear implication. An example of this can be seen in Turner's dome forms, where the logical continuation of the profile is two lines extending to meet at an apex at some point above the pot. Many of Susanne Stephenson's pots employ the same type of form.

A similar exercise can be carried out with DeVore's vessels. If we continue the lines of the foot, they converge at an invisible point below the surface on which the pot stands. These implied spaces are very real, if subconscious, elements in our perception of a vessel's form.

The third profile is most common in bowls and plates (other than those that suggest an orb) where the projected lines of the profile move away from each other and never intersect. In such forms the sense of projection is infinite, occupying an endless continuum of space. In a symbolic sense such vessels become containers of the universe, and it is not surprising that seemingly simple bowls and plates are so frequently the most spatially captivating objects.

Outside these three types of profiles are other derivations that are less frequent. In Kenneth Price's work the defining edge must be seen less as profile and more in three-dimensional terms. Here implied space is dealt with consciously and literally. The play between line and color to set up a dialectic with form has long been part of the visual language of this artist. The forms illustrated here began to appear in 1972, when Price produced a brilliant series of cup forms that employed a neo-Cubist format together with tough Art Deco styling.

These cups emphasized line through the hard-edged forms, the flat, bright color, and the tense, sharp edges delineated by a thin white line. The complex arrangement of angular projections from the main form echoed Umberto Boccioni's call in his 1912 *Manifesto of Futurist Sculpture* for form that went beyond a volumetric rendition of the object. In his work *The Spatial Dynamics of a Bottle*, Boccioni explored what he termed the "spatial milieu" that surrounds an object. In an extended sense, employing a teasing play between two and three dimensions, Price's cups and vessels explore the same issues.

Profile is less important in reading those works that are of an assemblage nature. Once a pot develops beyond two or more primary forms, new complexities enter the linear relationship. In the work of Woodman and Rothman, for instance, one is faced with line defining an inner sense of structure wherein each component enjoys independence, and the feet, necks, spouts, lids, and handles all clamor for attention and show little subservience to the main form.

Examination of the individual elements of the pottery aesthetic can become somewhat cold-blooded and didactic. Although it is helpful to dissect and examine the elements individually, we in fact rarely look at an object in so carefully indexed a manner. Line's most important role finally is a dynamic one, the kinetic binding of all elements that comprise the majesty of the vessel. In order to fully appreciate line in pottery we must add movement, as Rawson explains:

> Obviously, if we are to get the best out of a pot or, if we are potters ourselves, to put the most into it, we have to know how to read such movement patterns, or how to construct them. We must learn to see not with a single motionless glance, but with mobile, surveying attention which allows all other qualities of the pot's surface —color, texture, and so on—to attach themselves to the contour. . . . Ceramic forms embody and bind together the analogues from our experience, conveying them from mind to mind, from maker

to spectator, creating those formal metaphors and suggestions which are in essence ultimately kinetic. For such lines do things in relation to their format; their meanings can be best expressed in verbs such as "swoop," "float," "swerve," "dip." The contour does something similar in relation to the vertical axis of a pot. But paired contour lines, in limiting and qualifying each other, may combine to suggest actions quite unutterable in words; and the notional "activity" a three-dimensional linear surface represents is totally indescribable, though we can indeed appreciate it.[24]

Movement in pottery comes most frequently from the rising and falling rhythms of throwing or coiling, from the swirling circle of the lip and the interreaction of vertical profile and horizontal contours. For most potters this sense of movement is a crucial aesthetic goal. This importance given to movement, to physicality, encourages an analogy with performance art. Indeed, pottery seems to find itself more at ease with the descriptive language of dance and music than it does with that of the visual arts.

Voulkos's comments on dance and clay have already been recorded. Others, too, speak of this analogous relationship. Turner employs the ideas of dance in teaching students to understand their own occupation of space, and thereby to better understand form. Frimkess talks of finding the "choreography" of a pot, implying that for each form there is an ideal set of movements and rhythms in manipulating the clay and that the achievement of their precise order and economy of gesture will establish the power of a particular form.

The concept of a performance element in ceramic art is potent and credible. The making of a pot is after all a physical event requiring highly refined and disciplined skills. In the cases of Voulkos, Autio, Rothman, Woodman, Staffel, and Soldner, the evidence of direct, active manipulation of the clay is almost overpowering. So, too, is the aspect of repetition. In the time it takes a painter to create one work, a potter may create tens, even hundreds, of pieces. To the untrained eye these might seem identical, and the essential form may change little over several years. The same may be said of the dancer or musician, but each time they replay an established form, the repetitive quality of performance brings new information, new understanding and depth. Repetition is the root of a performer's finesse.

But to those who look closely enough, each performance is also different, providing new tonality, different moods, and changes in structural emphasis. It is evident from reviewing the work here that this concept is not a key to unlock the mysteries of all ceramic art. In the work of DeVore, Daley, Price, and Nagle the sense of performance is more muted, their work not being based on an aesthetic of intuitive action but on a more studied, cerebral examination of issues, mainly a questioning of the formal elements of the vessel on a conceptual level. Frimkess's works straddle both

areas, combining expressive throwing skills with a contextual device of satirizing vessels that we readily identify as the cultural archetypes of Chinese and Greek forms.

Finally in our discussion of ceramic aesthetics, it is necessary to explore the relationship of surface and form. This is by far the most complex area in the appreciation of the art. It is also beyond the scope of this essay to deal definitively with the topic. What I wish to achieve, however, is a clarification of some of the language and theory that relate to this subject.

In dealing with the surface, potters have a far greater variety of means at their disposal than even painters. Glazes can provide a wealth of effects: the liverish reds of *sang de boeuf* (copper reduction), dense matte colors, shimmering lusters, thick fatty whites, translucent celadon greens and grays, crystalline formations, and rainbow-hued iridescents. Glazes can resemble fur, can crackle, craze, crawl (withdraw from the clay surface), bubble, and erupt into a craterous surface. These can be used in endless combinations with relief decoration, drawing into wet clay, painting, trailing or feathering with wet slip, drawing through wet slip or glaze (sgraffito), photo-decal application, china painting on glaze, acid etching, incising, excising, sprigging (adding clay elements), chattering (turning lines on leather-hard clay), and scores of other techniques that potters have either added to their vocabulary in this century or gleaned from their art's long past.

The diversity of techniques (and an equal diversity of conceptual applications of those techniques) is extraordinarily broad, but the descriptive language is, by comparison, regrettably narrow. For the greater part, when the surface of a pot is being described, the term *decoration* is used. One can understand the use of such a catchall word in the face of the complex surface treatments, but mostly the term is used incorrectly, resulting, much as with the incorrect use of the term *craft*, in the obscuring of the artist's true motives.

George Woodman notes that there is no need for the term to be used incorrectly: "Decoration, unlike most notions in art, is clear and unambiguous. . . . We don't have to misuse it—one thing decorates another, serves to adorn, beautify or embellish another thing."[25] By comparison we never speak of a drawing as "decorating" a piece of paper, although we may see the drawing as being of a decorative style. In this book the same distinctions between *decorating* and *decorative* need to be made.

Much of the surface treatment here is unashamedly decorative. Ken Ferguson's black and green platter and Warren MacKenzie's finger-combed bowl come closest to being termed "decorated" pots. The artists frequently choose to leave similar forms unadorned, and the surface activity, although integrated, is not an essential part of the form's *raison d'être*—it is an option. Yet even if one does consider this to be decoration, effective decoration requires considerable sensitivity and should not be undervalued. As critic Amy Goldin admonished, "Good decoration may be intellectually empty but it need not be stupid."

Ferguson's and MacKenzie's works just cited fall into the area of emblematic decoration, which is the most common form of surface painting or drawing in ceramics. Its relationship to form is generally passive, complementing and not challenging its host form: "The essence of the graphic emblem is its flat character. It adheres, as it were, to the outer surface of the pot, implying no visible spaces which are not on the pot's own surface. It does not demand that we make an imaginative act which breaches the integrity of the plastic body."[26]

The use of an emblematic form of surface activity does not imply automatically that one is dealing with decoration. Paul Soldner's use of flat, stylized female forms (applied with the aid of a stencil) is obviously not an attempt to "decorate" a plaque or pot but is conceived in compositional terms in the same way as, say, Frank Stella creatively uses both surface and unconventionally framed canvases. The format (vessel) and surface are equally important statements. Yet Soldner's work is undoubtedly and unashamedly in a decorative mode (as that term applies to painting), as too is the work of John Glick and Betty Woodman.

One would hesitate, however, to apply the term *decorative* to the pottery of Voulkos, Staffel, or Turner, though the surfaces are embellished with marks. What separates their work from that of the emblematic-decorative school is related to Rawson's comment that such work should not breach "the integrity of the plastic body." In fact, all three do breach this integrity, both physically and imaginatively, through an energetic three-dimensional drawing that breaks down the passive accord between surface and form.

The Italian painter Lucio Fontana, who worked extensively in ceramics, was the first to introduce this form of surface action during the early 1950s, when he also slit and punctured his canvases. Voulkos began to use a similar vocabulary in the late 1950s and early 1960s, puncturing and tearing his plates and later adding pellets of porcelain. Although the result was still a plate, Slivka's characterization of these works as "clay drawings" is instructive: "[Voulkos] has penetrated the plane of the plate as though it were a sheet and given it light and space breathing through ragged crusted edges — we see through them to the next person, wall, object; or he introduces porcelain for emphasis and contradiction — to fill up the holes, give them another weight, another light. Air and/or porcelain evoke each other, set off each other, fulfill the same dimensional and volumetric function."[27]

The surface drawing of Staffel is as radical as, if not more radical than, that of Voulkos; it is certainly less

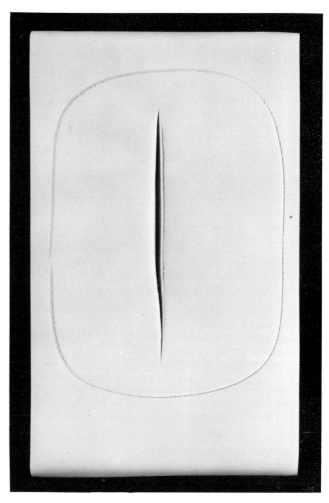

Concetto Spaziale by Lucio Fontana, Rosenthal China, Germany (1968), porcelain. Limited edition. Known primarily as a painter, Lucio Fontana began to explore the puncturing, cutting, and opening of plate or plaque surfaces in the early fifties. His ceramics (begun in 1934) constitute an important part of his oeuvre, and by the time of his death in 1968 he had become acknowledged as one of the most avant-garde figures in European ceramic art.

tied to classical form. Staffel achieves surface penetration of planes and volumes in two ways: first by overlapping small sections of porcelain of varying thicknesses to create a textured relief surface, and second by directing light into these "light gatherers." Where the porcelainous body is thinnest, the translucence is at its most intense; in places light almost destroys the materiality of the clay. As the clay sections overlap, so the translucence decreases, creating a tonal-planar surface built up through the play (what the Josef Hoffmann School refers to as the "push-pull") of light and shade.

Turner's surfaces are by comparison the most gentle of the three. The artist's comparison of his drawing on the pots with lines left by the ebb and flow of the tides on the fringe of a beach explains his philosophy. As Turner states, he will draw "only that which the clay will accept."[28] Turner's drawing involves several techniques: impressing patches of texture, applying long, thin slabs of clay to the pot surface, incising both lightly and deeply into the plastic surface, and stamping geometric forms to create new planes and emphasize the relationship of inner and outer spaces.

Many of the works here rely for their surface interest upon the seemingly random action of the kiln. I use the word *seemingly* advisedly, because the potter has considerable control as he or she becomes familiar with kiln and materials. This is an area of considerable myth and romance; the so-called looseness of these techniques — wood firing, raku, salt glazing, soda glazing, pit firing — is seductive.

Although it might seem that success depends upon the generosity of the kiln, these techniques require considerable control and finesse. Unfortunately, a generation has developed that confuses "being loose" (to use the potter's patois) with having decorative diarrhea. Spontaneity, paradoxically, springs most readily out of the most exacting discipline. The "unfocused play with materials" may be a goal in art, but it can only be achieved when the craft is not a conscious issue. The only way in which craft can become unconscious is through mastering one's materials and processes.

This "ease" of process in using the fire as a tool is apparent in many works shown here: in Karen Karnes's masterfully underplayed salt glazing; in Ferguson's rich, flowing wood-fired teapots; in Beatrice Wood's volatile use of inglaze luster; and in the recent plates by Voulkos that are fired in a Japanese-style kiln outside New York that maximizes ash flashing and flame marks. In Soldner's work the fire is most actively explored through the raku technique, involving an intimacy and immediacy in the use of the kiln.

The forms are first bisque fired, then painted, dipped, or sprayed with various glazes or oxides and plunged into a kiln for a few minutes, to be withdrawn with tongs and placed, glowing red, in a bin of straw, wet grass, or other material. The general effect can be predicted within a wide range of possibilities. But frequently the results are surprising, producing an endless range of colorful, rich, smoky surface patination. In such work, where the composition of the surface can be loosely directed but not fully controlled, the artist (or the public) has to edit carefully, for just as the kiln can be generous, so too can it mar the works it is presented.

In the work of Nagle and DeVore one seems to deal with the same "fortuitous" surface. But the casualness of these surfaces is in fact arrived at by a process of the most exacting control, involving as many as fifteen firings to realize the textures and strong bland colors. In Nagle's works even the highlights and touches of light one sees on the surface are in fact a china-painted illusion. With both artists what emerges from the final firing is entirely of their making. Unlike Voulkos,

Karnes, and Soldner, they never turn their works over to the kiln but employ it without romance as a finely calculated tool.

The problems of describing the ceramic surface stem largely from the number of techniques a potter may use on a single work. In the case of Rudy Autio, for instance, a pot incorporates sgraffito drawing, painting with both dry slips and high-gloss glazes, surface modeling, and incising. The surface further exists within a three-dimensional format of outline and contours that makes up the voluptuously anthropomorphic forms. There is no single term to explain the extreme complexity and sophistication of such work other than perhaps the term *potter's space.*

Our appreciation of such space is further limited by Western conventions in looking at a pot. By such standards Autio's work might seem awkward and incomplete. If we transfer our spatial allegiance to Eastern poles of thought, however, "based upon assumptions, intuitions, even a metaphysic . . . entirely foreign to the Western humanist tradition,"[29] such work becomes comprehensible as part of an environment without defined limits in which any painted or drawn object might appear without question. Rawson expands upon this concept that the French art historian Henri Focillon defines as *l'espace milieu:*

> The artist has no obligation to define a perspective-box, or to make his objects fit into the frame provided according to any formula save their own presence. The picture does not have to describe a complete visual field to be consistent. For even when there is only one feature on it, say a single figure, the picture space is already, as it were, complete and satisfactory in the pot surface; what the artist does is to materialize with his cursive brush those aspects of the phenomenon he considers worth rendering. He can quite happily allow parts of an object to "vanish" beyond the edge of the format as if it continued in space beyond it. For the pot's own space is continuous with the space around it, into which it extends and which makes it perceptible."[30]

Apart from the purely visual concerns already raised about the complexity of the potter's space, one can add the subject of color, its symbolism, our emotional response to it, and the even more involved impact of a polychromatic palette upon three-dimensional form. And yet how often do we hear pottery referred to as being a simple craft?

This leads me to recall a discussion passed on to me by Michael Cardew that took place in the early years of the Leach pottery in St. Ives. Leach and the twenty-ninth-generation Japanese Asahi potter Tsuranosuke Matsubayashi were examining a rough peasant bowl from Korea. Leach, in questioning how it had been made, remarked that the process must have been very simple. Matsubayashi smiled indulgently and countered, "No, I think it was very complicated." In truth, both were correct. It is between the seeming contradictions of simplicity and complexity that the mysterious essence of all ceramic art is centered.

IN CLOSING

The comments of writer and critic Clement Greenberg seem apropos in closing. During his keynote address at the Ceramic Symposium: 1979, Greenberg remarked about the hierarchies in art and the manner in which photography once faced the same challenge of acceptance as pottery:

> Well, is ceramics getting or going to get, as photography has, the benefit of a recent leveling of status? The question requires two different answers. The one has to do with opinion, the other with actual achievement, with aesthetic results. It seems to me that [ceramic art] is getting more serious attention of late. Attention is a matter of opinion. Is that what ceramists want most: favorable opinion? Are ceramists to bother about whether they are put down as potters or hailed as sculptors? Should they, and we, care about nomenclature? Opinion changes, achievement stays. Achievement also erases the difference between the utilitarian, the vessels, and fine art, sculpture. Once again, results—experienced, not discussed or debated—are all that count when it comes to art as art.[31]

Greenberg went on to suggest that the potter not despair of receiving recognition, but that this not be the goal. "There is nothing that says that a great pot cannot match a great statue in aesthetic importance," he concluded. "Let the vessel-maker show us that there are no rules or prescriptions or laid-down-in-advance categories of value in art."

I submit that Greenberg's advice be taken. Ceramics has for too long been submerged in a swamp of opinion. The endless debates of art versus craft, of functionalism and nonfunctionalism, are built on the shifting sands of opinion. The position of the vessel as art or nonart is similarly mere opinion. This will shift to the left and the right in coming decades with the vagaries of art theory and politics. We must therefore now consign our greatest effort dealing with achievement.

The vessels that are illustrated here constitute the major statement in this book about the success of the contemporary American potter. As self-conscious works of art (some potters might prefer the word *unconscious*), they can and must be judged by the rigorous visual and aesthetic criteria relevant to this medium. On this basis it becomes apparent that these twenty artists have greatly altered our perception of the vessel and enlarged upon pottery's millennia-long history.

NOTES

INTRODUCTION

1. Joan Simon, "An Interview with Ken Price," *Art in America* 68, no. 1 (January 1980): 97.

TRANSFORMATION AND INHERITANCE

1. André Malraux, *Les Voix du Silence* (Paris: Gallimard, 1951), p. 83.

2. Bernard Leach, "American Impressions," *Craft Horizons* 10 (Winter 1950).

3. William Morris, "The Lesser Arts of Life," in *Ceramic Art: Comment and Review, 1882–1977*, ed. Garth Clark (New York: E. P. Dutton, 1978), p. 14. "The Lesser Arts of Life" was first given as a lecture in Birmingham, England, on January 23, 1882.

4. Herbert Read, *Art and Industry* (London: Faber and Faber, 1935).

5. Morris, "The Lesser Arts of Life," p. 17.

6. For a fuller discussion of this early period in American ceramics and an overview of the modern movement, see Garth Clark, *A Century of Ceramics in the United States, 1878–1978* (New York: E. P. Dutton, 1979).

7. Robert Blasberg, *George E. Ohr and His Biloxi Pottery* (Port Jervis, N.Y.: J. W. Carpenter, 1972). For a discussion of the aesthetics of Ohr, see Garth Clark, "George E. Ohr — Clay Prophet," *Craft Horizons* 38 (October 1978).

8. Adelaide Robineau, "Ceramics at the Paris Exposition," *Design* 27–28 (December 1925–September 1926), a series of ten articles.

9. Glen Lukens, "The New Craftsman," *Design* 38 (May 1937).

10. "Ceramics: The Art with the Inferiority Complex," *Fortune* 16 (December 1937): 114.

11. Rose Slivka, "New Ceramic Presence," *Craft Horizons* 21 (July–August 1961).

12. Bernard Leach, "Belief and Hope," in *Ceramic Art*, ed. Clark, p. 88. The essay was first published in Bernard Leach, *50 Years a Potter* (London: Arts Council of Great Britain, 1961).

13. Philip Rawson, *Ceramics*, The Appreciation of the Arts, vol. 6 (London: Oxford University Press, 1971), p. 19.

14. Quoted by Bernard Leach in "Towards a Standard," the opening chapter of *A Potter's Book* (London: Faber and Faber, 1940).

15. Edy de Wilde, introduction to *West Coast Ceramics* (Amsterdam: Stedelike Museum, 1979).

16. See Herbert Read, *The Meaning of Art* (London: Faber and Faber, 1931), pp. 41–42.

17. Kenneth W. Jones, "Richard E. DeVore," *Philadelphia Arts Exchange* 1 (March–April 1977).

18. Rawson, *Ceramics*, p. 206. As Rawson is quoted frequently in this essay, it seems necessary to say more about his book, which is probably the only study in any depth of the theory of pottery aesthetics. It is an excellent work recommended to those who wish to research this subject in greater detail. Its shortcomings are that it deals mainly with the period up to the eighteenth century and only glancingly with the modern movement, and there is an overall bias toward the painted pot. The more expressionist vocabulary of monochrome ware and the Zen pottery of Japan is dealt with all too briefly.

19. George Woodman, "Ceramic Decoration and the Concept of Ceramics as Decorative Art," a paper read on June 2, 1979, at the Ceramics Symposium: 1979 in Syracuse, New York. The paper is published in *Transactions of the Ceramic Symposium: 1979*, ed. Garth Clark (Los Angeles: Institute for Ceramic History, 1980).

20. Leach, pp. 87–88.

21. Interview with Voulkos by Garth Clark, February 14, 1980, at the Dome in Oakland, California.

22. Michael Cardew, "Why Make Pots in the Last Quarter of the 20th Century?" *Studio Potter* 7, no. 1 (1978): 46–47.

23. Cardew, "Why Make Pots," p. 47.

24. Rawson, *Ceramics*, pp. 110–111.

25. Woodman, "Ceramic Decoration."

26. Rawson, *Ceramics*, p. 159.

27. Rose Slivka, "The New Clay Drawings of Peter Voulkos," *Craft Horizons* 34 (October 1974): 31.

28. Clark, *A Century of Ceramics*, p. 335.

29. Rawson, *Ceramics*, p. 183.

30. *Ibid.*

31. Clement Greenberg, "Status of Clay," a paper read on June 1, 1979, at the Ceramics Symposium: 1979 in Syracuse, New York. The paper is published in *Transactions of the Ceramic Symposium: 1979*, ed. Clark.

AMERICAN POTTERS

THE WORK OF TWENTY MODERN MASTERS

RUDY AUTIO

Rudy Autio was born in Butte, Montana, in 1926 and studied at Montana State University, Bozeman (B.S. 1950), and Washington State University, Pullman (B.F.A. 1952). After graduating, he became the resident artist at the Archie Bray Foundation in Helena, Montana, where he worked with Peter Voulkos (then also fresh from graduate school). Autio developed an interest in architectural works and completed several commissions, including a 30-foot ceramic wall for the First Methodist Church, Great Falls, Montana. After leaving the Bray Foundation in 1957, Autio joined Montana State University in Bozeman as professor of ceramics and sculpture.

From the early sixties his interest in figurative themes became apparent. *Double Lady Vessel* (1964), which is in the collection of the Everson Museum of Art, and an untitled luster-painted vase (1968) in the Marer Collection at Scripps College are early and excellent examples of this exploration. At first examination the painted surfaces of Autio's work recall something of the style of the Fauve ("wild beast") painters of Europe and in particular Henri Matisse, Cornelius van Dongen, and Maurice Vlaminck. But upon further examination, this initial impression proves to be superficial.

Granted, Autio uses an existing language in his drawing of voluptuous figurative form, but in partnership with clay this is pushed beyond stylistic categorization. The ragged drawing into the surface of the vessels, the overlapping slabs of clay, and the three-dimensionality excite a particularly raw strength and energy that have something of the spirit and intensely personal, nonformalist quality of Jean Dubuffet's Art Brut.

The employment of the vessel as a host for figurative imagery has a long tradition in Western ceramics. Autio takes his place with the best of the modern exponents of the genre (if it can be seen as a collective entity): Wallace Martin, Paul Gauguin, Sam Haile, William Staite Murray, Henry Varnum Poor, Pablo Picasso, Marc Chagall, and others. And yet Autio's work has received comparatively little public attention. This has been in part the result of Autio's modesty, his geographic isolation from the main art centers, and his small, intermittent output (about twenty vessels a year). Although general acclaim has been slow in developing, Autio does enjoy the unqualified respect of his peers as one of the major forces and talents in defining an American aesthetic for the vessel.

Autio's pots are bisque fired in a gas kiln at cone 4 to 5 and then refired at cone 08. Slips or engobes are applied on the damp greenware, after which the surface is drawn through and then sprayed with a fine film of Gerstley borate glaze to give a sheen. Bright low-fire glazes are painted and dabbed on after the bisque firing. The clay body is composed of a half-and-half mixture of fire clay and ball clay, with some earthenware clay, grog, and chopped fiber added. The latter provides strength to the plastic clay while the vessels are being slab built.

VAL CUSHING

Val Murat Cushing was born in Rochester, New York, and was educated at the New York State School of Clayworking and Ceramics at Alfred University (B.F.A. 1952; M.F.A. 1956). He taught briefly at the University of Illinois, Urbana, and directed the summer school in pottery at Alfred University from 1957 to 1965. He is now a professor of pottery at Alfred University and works from his studio in Alfred Station. Cushing has been active in other areas of the ceramic arts: as chairman of the standards committee of New York State Craftsmen and chairman of the technical committee of the National Council for Education in the Ceramic Arts from 1962 to 1966.

Cushing's work has been consistent throughout his career—in the gentle curving lines, the sunken domed lids, and the sense of enclosure that distinguish his oeuvre. He produces various forms: bowls, casseroles, and lidded jars. It is the latter, however, that have become his most distinctive format.

In looking at Cushing's work, one does not expect conceptual preoccupations, provocative form, or any bending of the rules of ceramic art. Cushing's stance is that of both Minimalist and traditionalist, defining and redefining a limited form vocabulary. The statement that emerges is gentle, understated, almost anonymous, in the same way folk art is.

His aesthetic is based upon nuances in the play within the form limitations Cushing has set for himself: his ability to achieve monumentality with great economy of form, his evident and finely tuned sense of craftsmanship, and the spatial interplay of the womblike vessels. In a contemporary sense it is a continuation of the ideal that the founder of the New York State School of Clayworking and Ceramics, Charles F. Binns, had proposed in his "less-is-more" aesthetic, except that with Cushing we find none of Binns's puritanism, but in its place a gentle coaxing of the vessel's tendency toward Minimalist form.

Cushing fires his pottery in a natural-gas kiln, bisque firing at cone 06 and glaze firing at cone 9 in a reduction atmosphere. The clay body he uses is composed of equal parts of fire clay, stoneware clay, and red clay with flint, and a small quantity of grog. Cushing uses several glazes but is particularly well known for his excellent aventurine glazes, which he describes as "Amber Celadon." The speckling that occurs in some of his pieces comes from the quantities of iron and manganese in the clay body.

WILLIAM DALEY

William Daley was born in Hastings-on-Hudson, New York, in 1925. He studied at the Massachusetts College of Art, Boston, and Columbia University Teachers College, New York City (M.Ed. 1951). Thereafter he taught at various schools in Iowa, New York, New Mexico, and, since 1966, at the Philadelphia College of Art, where he heads the ceramics department.

Daley's early work was based upon Chinese ritual bronzes, in particular Shang bells with their ellipsoidal cross sections and scooped rims. Daley was attracted to these works because of their powerful simplicity and spatial presence. These qualities he has sought in his own work ever since, attempting to capture the essence of the bronzes without literally imitating them.

Unhappy with the potter's wheel, Daley soon developed a distinctive technique of hand-building his pots upside down on a plaster form or hump (he now uses Styrofoam). As he worked in this manner, Daley realized his pots were different spatially from most. Although upside down, the outer form was perfectly clear, whereas the inner form remained ambiguous until removed from the plaster hump on which it was formed. Once the pot was right side up, this relationship changed.

The inside of the pot could be seen at a glance. But the outer wall of the pot, because of the overhanging edge, complex structure, and viewing angle (Daley's pots are mostly conceived as floor pieces), could not be perceived as easily and had to be viewed from several different positions to establish its shape. Furthermore, even though the inner and outer walls were direct positive-negative shapes, the complexity of the forms rendered this relationship unclear. Inner and outer forms, instead of possessing the unity of conventional pottery, seem to exist independent of one another; the connections of negative and positive are far from apparent to the casual viewer.

Finally, like some exercise in perspectival illusion, they do finally merge. But achieving this visual marriage demands careful visual analysis of the forms. This complexity is due in part to the often ignored fact that there is a difference in area between the inner and outer walls (the latter being the greater) and that the resultant difference in scale is actually perceptible when we consciously acknowledge it. This greatly alters the formal relationship between the two sides of the shared wall.

In an address at the National Council on Education for the Ceramic Arts conference in 1979, Daley spoke of this, remarking that he had begun to play with multiple exits and entrances in his work to make "chambers and ditches that went through or around the pots . . . attempting to use the edge to control the sense of open and closed; sometimes outside segments had large negative sections to suggest they might be inside a greater space."

A guest lectureship in New Mexico in 1972 brought Daley to another important departure point. He visited sites of early Pueblo potteries and examined collections of the pots themselves as well. To Daley these dramatic black and white vessels spoke of his own obsession with negative and positive space. When he returned to the East he attempted to translate the designs on Pueblo pottery into three dimensions, noting that "the steps and zigzags were marvelous building structures when three-dimensional, recapitulating earlier play with modules, bumps, and patterns—from pummeled clay surfaces to Iowa tractor treads and worm gears." Since then a new sensitivity, both spatial and compositional, has enlivened his work.

Daley's work now deals with a "structure of pattern and the way it defines space" that is essentially architectonic in concept. This is a relatively new tradition in the West, where pottery has been dominated by wheel-thrown (or coiled) symmetry in the classical style. The roots of a style more concerned with building structures and with the articulation of the individual components goes back to the turn of the century in the Austro-Hungarian Empire, when architects and designers such as Josef Hoffmann, Koloman Moser, Joseph Maria Olbrich, Vlastislav Hofman, and Emile Pichan began to explore a constructivist, geometric approach to the vessel. Daley is one of the contemporary inheritors of that search, and he has managed to enlarge its dimensions and spatial content, not only in pottery but in the many large-scale architectural commissions he has undertaken throughout the United States.

RICHARD DEVORE

Richard DeVore was born in Toledo, Ohio, in 1933. He studied at the University of Toledo (B.Ed. 1955) and under Maija Grotell (1899–1973) at Cranbrook Academy of Art, Bloomfield Hills, Michigan (M.F.A. 1957). After a period of teaching at Michigan's Flint Junior College, DeVore was chosen by Grotell to head the ceramics department at Cranbrook upon her retirement. He taught there from 1966 to 1978, when he moved to Colorado State University, Fort Collins.

At the time DeVore joined Cranbrook, however, he was still in a very exploratory phase, producing pinch-necked bottles with leatherlike surfaces, slab-built lanterns, brightly glazed pots on legs, and sculptural pieces such as luster-painted male torsos. From about 1969 forms began to appear that have become, with slight changes, the central thrust of his work: shallow bowls and tall vase forms. Writing in *The New Art Examiner*, Andy Nasisse concluded that "DeVore's containers are androgynous; the various heights allow a versatility of presentation, some related to the male principle, others to the female," adding that the opposition of feminine (light) and masculine (dark) is inherent in DeVore's use of color as well.

The male-female polarity is basic to the formal vocabulary of all potters, but in DeVore's work this interplay is particularly noticeable, as his vessels deal simultaneously with expansive and contractive space. This duality is particularly evident in his bowls, whose walls are pierced by small holes. Depending upon the lighting, these holes seem light against dark on one side, dark against light on the other. In this sense a DeVore pot is not unlike the male-female *t'ai-chi* symbol, with its pinpoints of light and dark.

The male-female, light-dark contrasts are not the only polarities in a DeVore pot. Equally important is the conflict between *techne* and *psyche*, rationality and intuition. DeVore attempts to find rational structure for emotion and in so doing sets up an unexpected tension. This tension is surprising only because of the initial impression of serenity his pots make on us; closer examination reveals an extraordinary degree of spatial turbulence.

This turbulence is deliberate. DeVore is not seeking what he terms "brutal anxiety," but rather "a matter-of-fact confrontation with a state of emotional existence that is reality to me." Much of this tension comes from the reductive process—the tuning and retuning of lines, surfaces, and proportions to achieve the most essential visual relationships. But in part the tension is also structural, resulting from the fact that all DeVore's pots strain to be frontal. This is achieved in part by lowering the front of the rim and raising the back. Activity at the back of the pot—whether color, movement, or detail of form—conspires to produce a surge of energy to the front. "To some degree," says DeVore, "these pots defy the security of that volume and space that is inside. There is a tension present, a pressure of the back trying to move forward. You have the dichotomous feeling that the bowl is three-dimensional and yet that it is trying to pull itself into a two-dimensional relationship."

The pots, unquestionably contemporary, communicate a sense of continuity with the potter's past, although that relationship is not specific. DeVore plays with all of the formal elements of the vessel: mass, volume, line, implied space, color, and surface texture. He draws the rims of his pots as though they are question marks, and in a sense they are. For the rim, more than any other element, is the point of access to DeVore's geometric sense of structure. Finally, DeVore infuses the pot with an intense, personal anthropomorphism that tempers its abstract qualities. The sensual surfaces—veined and skinlike—the thin membranes at the bottom of his bowls, the tautness of the curved walls, all speak of the human body and, more pointedly, of man and woman as sexual beings.

DeVore fires his work in an electric kiln, bisque firing at cone 08 to 04 and glaze firing between cone 6 and 9. The pot then undergoes several additional firings between cone 05 and 03. After each, new glazes are brushed on to develop the crackle by causing surface tension. This process is repeated for up to twenty firings. The bottom 2 inches of DeVore's pots are thrown dry and hand-built from there on. DeVore uses a natural stoneware clay (Pine Lake) combined with Redart clay for plasticity. The final step is to wrap the pots in oil-soaked newspaper; the package is then set alight and plunged into a lidded drum and a high-pressure reduction atmosphere is created.

KENNETH FERGUSON

Kenneth Ferguson was born in Elwood, Indiana. He studied at the summer school of the American Academy of Art, Chicago, the Carnegie Institute in Pittsburgh (B.F.A. 1952), and the New York State School of Clayworking and Ceramics at Alfred University (M.F.A. 1954). Ferguson has taught at various institutions, including the Carnegie Institute, Alfred University, and the Archie Bray Foundation, Helena, Montana. In the early 1960s he joined the Kansas City Art Institute and there developed its ceramics department into one of the major centers for pottery education in the United States.

Over the years certain aspects of Ferguson's work have changed, while others have remained constant. He has continued to be a traditionalist, and his works deal primarily with utility. He enjoys the discipline of being a production potter—throwing, glazing, decorating, and firing hundreds of mixing bowls, tea bowls, teapots, baskets, lidded jars, and bowls every year—and this is how he prefers to be viewed. His exhibition at the William Rockhill Nelson Gallery of Art in Kansas City, "The Three Kilns of Ken Ferguson," comprised 201 objects selected from firings over the preceding six months. The selection was to some extent indiscriminate. He did not screen out all but the masterworks; he honestly presented all that a potter might make: the dazzling successes, the workmanlike pieces that make up most of the output, and even a few of the failures.

The exhibition also underlined the manner in which Ferguson has developed a distinctive style over the years. Early works from the sixties betrayed a certain brittle quality. The forms were strong, the dry surfaces compelling, but the pottery lacked feeling. Twenty years later that criticism cannot be made. Ferguson's pots are powerful emotionally and viscerally—the tangible, concrete responses of an artist coming to terms with himself and his feelings. In the process, his forms have lost some of the heroic monumentality that earlier characterized them while gaining intimacy in its place.

Above all, Ferguson's pottery is enlivened by an underlying eroticism. The term may seem inappropriate to describe seemingly staid traditional pottery—vessels replete with references to Oribe wares and other Japanese influences of the past—yet this quality remains. The manner in which the forms tend to slump in the center, the rudely protuberant spouts, creased and loosely formed, create an anthropomorphic quality that is exceedingly intimate. We are reminded not only of the human form, but of the details: folds of voluptuous flesh swelling, sagging, creasing at the joints.

This eroticism is surprisingly less persuasive in his painted platters and bowls depicting nude figures, where the statement is too direct to carry the layers of metaphor. The finest of these, however, are his *Adam and Eve* plates, drawn with a sense of humor and keen appreciation of potter's space. They are the kind of drawings that, if transferred to paper, simply would not live; in partnership with the vessel form, however, they possess true decorative vitality. They are the Thomas Toft plates of our day—fresh, brusquely economical, and born of man's insatiable urge to paint, draw, pattern, or otherwise leave his mark upon the vessel.

Ferguson fires three kilns, two gas kilns outside Kansas City (one salt glaze, the other stoneware reduction) and a two-chamber wood-burning kiln at his summer studio in Centennial, Wyoming. He fires most of his work at cone 10 to 11. The stoneware clay body is a mixture of Chicago Wellsville, Goldart, Pine Lake, and Missouri fire clays, together with Spink ball clay, Custer feldspar, and less than 1 percent red iron oxide. The porcelain is composed of Crolleg china clay, Custer feldspar, flint, Pyrotol, and 2½ percent bentonite. Ferguson uses a wide range of decorating techniques, including painting with slip and glazes, but he relies most upon creative use of the fire.

MICHAEL FRIMKESS

Michael Frimkess was born in Los Angeles in 1937. At the age of fifteen he was admitted to the Los Angeles County Art Institute (now the Otis/Parsons Art Institute), where he studied sculpture. One night, spurred on by the vision while on a peyote trip of throwing a giant pot, Frimkess decided to join the ceramics department, then chaired by Peter Voulkos. He was one of the last students to join, but he rapidly became an important force in the "Otis" group.

Like many of his contemporaries, Frimkess also worked in disciplines other than clay. He created multimedia iconographic assemblages and bronze sculpture, such as the television-set sculpture *Hooker* (1962). After 1965, however, the vessel became the dominant format for his work. The symbolism he uses relates to his childhood and the experience of "being the last Jewish family left in Boyle Heights." He grew up with Chicano, Japanese, and black children and in that environment developed his ideal of the "melting pot": a peaceful, homogeneous potpourri of the world's many cultures, colors, and religions.

A Frimkess pot, therefore, is ideologically not unlike an Edward Hicks canvas of *The Peaceable Kingdom*. The lexicon is different, though, revealing the roughness of a street-wise artist. Frimkess's drawing has the quality of graffiti; the images are urgent, raw, and often incomplete. His forms are derived from known classical models that function as the cultural

archetype: Chinese ginger jars, Greek Panathenic amphorae, Zuñi Indian pottery.

His ambition is to create the ultimate melting pot: "I want to complete the pun and put together all my research over the years into a melting pot—a pile of different cultures in one work. Each culture will be represented by a classic, ethnic shape, all piled on top of one another, all working together as one pot that will be a functional piece for smoking pot. That's the second pun."

Technique, or more accurately, process, is important to Frimkess. A period of working in a Pennsylvania commercial pottery, where the Italian potter he replaced had thrown without water, led Frimkess to believe that this was the way Greek amphorae had been produced. He spent several months at New York's Metropolitan Museum of Art and Boston's Museum of Fine Arts exploring this thesis; upon his return to California he began working in this manner.

Reverence for the Greek potter is a constant theme in his work. In a 1966 article in *Craft Horizons*, entitled "The Importance of Being Classical," he paid homage to Greek culture, stating somewhat controversially, "The Greek and Chinese potters had one thing in common; both cultures developed classic forms which corresponded to their practical uses, but the Greeks at the highest point of their culture were by far the best throwers ever to dig clay from this earth."

Throwing for Frimkess acquires an importance beyond technique. It represents for the artist what the mantra represents for the Hindu—a means of self-release. As Frimkess has said, "Wheel throwers remain philosophers, humanitarians, and men of conscience, aware of their time's mission, ever on a par with the great sculptors, perfectionist painters, writers and musicians. Due to throwing's freedom-giving limitations, it is still one of the best roads to self improvement. . . . The potter communicates with the clay through control and knows the consequences if communication is lost."

Until recently Frimkess has been firing his pots in a downdraft gas kiln in Venice, built several years ago for Michael Cardew when he was in Los Angeles working on a film about his pottery. The pots are bisque fired at cone 06 to 05 and glaze fired at cone 10 to 11. China-painted surfaces are fired between cone 015 and 022. Frimkess used some "hobby shop" glazes as well as a black and white stoneware glaze that he has developed. Pots are thrown dry, frequently in one piece, enabling Frimkess to produce extremely light, finely tuned forms. The technique results in a high mortality rate, however; fewer than half the works survive firing.

JOHN GLICK

Born in Detroit, Michigan, in 1938, John Parker Glick studied at Wayne State University (B.F.A. 1960) and at Cranbrook Academy of Art, Bloomfield Hills, Michigan (M.F.A. 1962). After two years in the United States Army he set up Plum Tree Pottery in Farmington, Michigan, producing hand-thrown utilitarian wares.

Glick's interest in functional pottery dates from his Wayne State days under William Pitney. This interest grew at Cranbrook, where he devoted his master's thesis to a study of the interchange between maker and user. This remains his concern today. Writing in *The Studio Potter: A Question of Quality*, Glick remarked, "If I were searching for a perfect counterpart to the pleasures making the wares give me, it would certainly have to be hearing from people who find special pleasure in their daily use and who seem to clearly sense the enjoyment the making of it provided me."

In this regard Glick's craft philosophy is similar to that of Roger Fry, the noted English art theoretician (and a potter himself during the years 1913–1918) who promulgated the following two dicta: that the artist can find functional expression for his genius; that an object can have no life or transcendent value unless it exhibits a "sense of joy in the making."

The combination of responsibility and exuberance that Glick feels for his role as a functional potter is evident in his work, which fuses formal design and playful decoration. The inspiration for these energetic surfaces comes from Japan, but the result is far from imitative. One senses Glick's ineluctable ties to Western culture. In particular, the free, almost calligraphic play with white lines of slip is reminiscent of Mark Tobey's White Writing and other gestures of the Abstract Expressionist school.

Unlike most potters, who must rely upon either the slightly barbarous system of juried fairs or the craft shop/gallery circuit in order to market their wares, Glick sells the bulk of his pottery from his own showroom. His sense of service, his understanding of the user's needs, is therefore acutely tuned.

Over the past ten years the production of dinner services, each created according to the individual needs of the family concerned, has become one of his principal modes of work. This is an arduous discipline few potters happily undertake. But Glick relishes the challenge, both physical and creative, and the response of his clients has been ample reward. Ten years ago he stopped showing place settings in his showroom to discourage new orders. Today there is a seven-year wait for a Glick service.

Glick pottery is not expensive. A setting of top-of-the-line European china costs almost ten times the price. This is not a deliberate policy of egalitarianism, however, and Glick does not consider who may or may not be able to afford the work. The pots "must be made first for themselves," he states, "because not to do so would be totally unsatisfying. . . . What will become of them is then seen more clearly in a perspective less to do with market considerations as a motivating force and more to do with a way of communicating feelings person to person."

Glick reduction fires his bisque wares at cone 09 and his glazed wares at cone 11 in a natural-gas kiln. The stoneware body is a mixture of Cedar Heights Gold Art (air-floated Ohio clay), Old Mine No. 4 ball clay, AP Green Missouri clay, grog, feldspar, and flint. Surface treatment is complex. Two to three slips are applied while the wares are green. The forms are imprinted and textured. Some of the imprinting takes place when the clay is so hard that only the most shallow and subtle indentation is recorded. Later, once glazed, the play of light on these areas creates a subtle texture. After the bisque firing another two to four slips are used. The glazes are selected from twelve formulas, varied with five to six color gradations. Forming processes are diverse. The wheel is the major tool, but an extruder is used for boxes, and wood and plaster molds for soap dishes.

KAREN KARNES

Karen Karnes was born in New York City in 1920. She first studied ceramics at the Newark School of Industrial Arts in New Jersey, having transferred from a disappointing architecture course. After a period of study at the New York State School of Clayworking and Ceramics at Alfred University, she and David Weinrib (her husband at the time) ran the pottery at Black Mountain College, near Asheville, North Carolina, from 1952 to 1954.

At Black Mountain (initially a hostile environment for the "crafts") she and Weinrib organized an important symposium attended by Bernard Leach, Shoji Hamada, and Soetsu Yanagi and moderated by the Bauhausler Marguerite Wildenhain. In 1954 Karnes moved to an artists' cooperative at Stony Point, New York, where she remained until 1979. Karnes is currently homesteading in Vermont, where she has the use of a wood-fired kiln, prior to leaving the United States for a new home and studio in Wales, Great Britain.

About twelve years ago she began to salt glaze her wares and has become internationally known for her accomplished use of this firing technique. Since her move from Stony Point, however, this type of work has come to an end. Most of the pieces illustrated here are from her final salt glaze firing at Stony Point.

In common with Price and Glick, Karnes has remained staunchly independent of the educational establishment. Although she occasionally participates in workshops, Karnes is determined to earn her living solely from making functional pottery. She draws her inspiration from traditionalist potters such as Shoji Hamada, requiring for herself the craftsman's discipline of daily contact with her materials and tools. The works themselves, however, are far from being romantic imitations of past cultures or times. The vessels could have been made in no century but our own.

Her traditionalism is that of which Michael Cardew spoke when he noted that those who call themselves traditionalists in fact do little more than take measurements of the work of the past, whereas the true traditionalist grows from an appreciation of the universal past of his or her art. Growth and change for Cardew, as for Karnes, are the life forces of traditionalism. Typical of this search for constant personal development is Karnes's decision to set aside her achievements in salt glazing, where she has established a very special place for herself, and take on new materials, new techniques, and a new culture.

This trenchant individualism marks all that she does. Although she sees herself primarily as a potter making functional vessels, she also works in clay on a large scale, making coil-built ovens and chairs. All the work shows a common hand, however. Volume is conceived of in an extremely controlled yet plastic manner; subtle waists, contours, and turned lines draw the viewer's attention to the powerful distribution of the contained space in each vessel. The pots simultaneously evoke both the gentleness and repose of the classical vessel and the dynamism, pressure, and tension of the centrifugal force that brought them into being.

Karnes salt fired the works illustrated here in a 45-cubic-foot, downdraft, natural-gas kiln at around cone 11 in a slightly reduced atmosphere. The clay body is composed of Grolleg china clay, fire clay, grog, and sand (the latter tends to increase the flocking effect on the surface and the sheen of the salt glaze). All the work is thrown, usually in one piece. She is now working in West Danville, Vermont, firing in a 100-cubic-foot, downdraft, wood kiln.

WARREN MACKENZIE

Warren MacKenzie, born in Kansas City in 1924, graduated from the Art Institute of Chicago (1947). He and his wife, Alix (1922–1962), spent the years 1949 to 1952 as apprentices to Bernard Leach in St. Ives, England. Shortly after their return to the United States, they established a pottery on a farm near Stillwater, Minnesota, where MacKenzie still works. Since 1954 MacKenzie has been the head of the ceramics department at the University of Minnesota.

When the MacKenzies returned to the United States in 1952, there was little serious interest in the functionalist views of either Leach or Michael Cardew. The fashionable or known U.S. potters of the prewar period were concerned mainly with producing individual pots. Only a few saw viable creative expression in a rigorous country workshop atmosphere. The functional spirit was kept precariously alive by the work of relatively unknown craftsmen such as Ben Owen (master potter of Jugtown Pottery in North Carolina), Bill Smith, and others who produced fully formed, utilitarian wares in the artisanal potteries of the southeastern section of the country.

The MacKenzies, quietly but persuasively, began to promulgate their ideals. In 1952 Alix organized the now legendary U.S. tour of Leach, Shoji Hamada, and Soetsu Yanagi that was to affect so profoundly the direction of American pottery in the following decade. The trio drew large audiences throughout the country.

Since then MacKenzie has become one of the leading spokesmen in the United States for the functional potter. He has lectured and demonstrated throughout the country, and he played a major role in the development of the National Council for Education in Ceramic Arts (NCECA). In his work MacKenzie has remained true to the disciplines of the country potter. His wares are simple one-piece forms (except for teapots), brusquely decorated, produced in large quantities (if somewhat sporadically), casually edited, and most modestly priced.

Pottery of this kind does not surrender its qualities easily. The outward appearance of simplicity can easily be mistaken for a dearth of content. But this has been true of most of the finest functional wares through the ages. There is an anonymity and minimalism that can be penetrated only through intimacy of use. MacKenzie explained this in a statement published in 1958 ("Ceramics: Double Issue," *Design Quarterly* 42–43), which has remained instructive as to his aesthetic stance: "Vitality of form is not limited because [a pot] will be used during a meal. The craft of pottery is dependent upon the physical contact of the observer and in handling, washing, drinking from, moving . . . the sensuous tactile qualities of clay and glaze can be understood in a manner which is different from the more distantly observed appreciation of a painting or piece of sculpture.

"A pot must be made with an immediacy, without unlimited change being possible, which is unique in the visual arts. For this reason each piece, in a sense, becomes a sketch or a variation of an idea which may develop over hours, days or months and require ten to several hundred pieces in order to come to full development. One pot suggests another, proportions are altered, curves are filled out or made more angular, a different termination or beginning of a line is tried—not searching for the perfect pot but exploring and making statements with the language at hand. From thousands of pots produced some few may sing. The others are sound stepping stones to these high points and can also communicate between the artist and user."

MacKenzie fires in a two-chamber downdraft gas kiln (propane). Bisque is fired at cone 01, and glaze firing (because of the unevenness of the kiln) ranges from cone 5 to cone 12. Most of the wares illustrated here have been fired between cones 10 and 12. The stoneware body is composed of Cedar Heights Air Floated, Old Hickory ball clay, feldspar, silica, and sand. The porcelain body is composed of Grolleg china clay, feldspar, silica, and a handful of ocher. Glazes are mainly of the feldspathic type.

RON NAGLE

Ron Nagle was born in San Francisco in 1939. He studied at San Francisco State University (B.A. 1962). In 1959 he met Peter Voulkos (who had then just begun to teach at the University of California, Berkeley) and was strongly influenced by the so-called Abstract Expressionist ceramics movement. This is evident in his *Bottle with a Stopper* (1960) in the Marer Collection at Scripps College, which shows an early interest in both color and stylized ceramic form.

In 1962 Nagle and Jim Melchert began to teach at the San Francisco Art Institute, completely redirecting the department from the then prevalent stoneware aesthetic to low-fired ceramics, which at the time was considered a medium appropriate only for hobbyists. (A year earlier Nagle had begun to work seriously with china paints and low-fired clay.) Both Nagle and Melchert had a strong and formative influence on the development of Bay Area ceramics and the low-fire movement nationwide — a debt that has yet to be fully acknowledged.

The influences on Nagle's work range from seventeenth-century Japanese wares of the Momoyama period (which he first became acquainted with in the classes of Henry Takemoto in the late 1950s) to the fetish-finish style of the Los Angeles School (Larry Bell, Billy Al Bengston, Robert Irwin, Kenneth Price, and others). In this regard Ken Price has been his most consistent inspiration, even mentor. Michael Frim-

kess was also influential during the early sixties; Nagle admired its unpredictability in particular.

Nagle recalls his pleasure at finding an alternative to the "blood-and-guts" school of the Abstract Expressionists. He found Price "making these little Grandma wares with bright colors on them . . . a little goofier, a little less macho—totally left field." In common with Price's work, Nagle's forms seem intended to be viewed from a single vantage point at a time, underscoring the pure line of their profiles. As Sylvia Brown has commented, "Nagle uses symmetry, both in the form and the painted schema, to encourage a view of the piece from the side, where the silhouette creates a linear image drawn between positive and negative space." In these graphic profiles Nagle strives for the looseness of a Morandi drawing while seeking the "tough and tender look" of Japanese wares. By this he means the seventeenth-century Momoyama wares to which he paid homage in his *Yama* series.

The cup, now Nagle's only format, has evolved over the past twenty years to a highly stylized form. The handle has become ever more conventionalized, appearing in "vestigial" form as a spur or fracture in the tense, controlled line of the cup's profile.

It is fair to say, however, that Nagle's pieces are not cups, but are *about* cups, which recalls Camilla Grey's comment about the Kasimir Malevich teapot for the Leningrad State Porcelain Factory: "not a teapot, but the idea of a teapot." Defining this work is problematic, existing as it does upon the cusp of many different disciplines—painting, sculpture, pottery, drawing.

Although pottery's past inspires Nagle, his gaze is not sentimentally fixed on its traditions. His work is tough, uncompromisingly contemporary, and draws upon the California palette of sunsets, oranges, swimming pools, and the spattered pink-and-black linoleum of the fifties. Because his is an active songwriter, music influences his work as well, and he recently established his own sound company, Proud Pork Productions. Alongside his recording studio in San Francisco is his newly constructed ceramics workshop. Nagle sees no difference between his music and his pottery, saying that he carries "lyrics and color chips in the same bag . . . they're both emotional, warm, and romantic; they're abstract and semislick; they both have flash and style; but I'm also shooting for content."

Nagle fires his cups in an electric kiln, bisque firing at cone 05 to 04 and glaze firing at cone 08 to 06. The body is earthenware composed of equal parts of ball clay and talc. The cups are put through ten to fifteen china paint firings at gradually reduced temperatures in the range of cone 015 to 022.

KENNETH PRICE

Kenneth Price was born in Los Angeles in 1935. He studied at the Chouinard Art Institute (1953–1954), the University of Southern California (B.F.A. 1956), with Peter Voulkos at the Otis Art Institute (until 1958), and at the New York State School of Clayworking and Ceramics at Alfred University (M.F.A. 1960).

Upon his return to Los Angeles, Price was given a one-man exhibition at the Ferus Gallery. Thereafter his work began to lose the casual playfulness of the Abstract Expressionistic works he had developed at Otis. For a time he set aside the vessel format and produced small, egglike sculptures painted in bright, acid colors that extended the surrealist vocabulary of such sculptors as Jean Arp and Constantin Brancusi. The works drew attention to the use of color in sculpture, influencing a nascent metal polychrome sculpture movement, and were among the earliest examples of a new style that brought a hard-edged finesse, the so-called fetish finish, to California art.

In the mid-sixties Price began to explore the cup again, both graphically in drawings and prints and three-dimensionally, as in *California Snail Cup* (1965). The most sophisticated development of this theme came between 1972 and 1974, however. Critic Mary King remarked in 1976 that Price had succeeded in taking a practical form—the cup—and transforming it by "a dizzying shift of spatial gears. Like a ball in an enclosed court the spectator bounces off ideas of the humble cup into the rarefied sophistication of Frank Stella reincarnated in 3-D, with persistent changes of scale wherein the curiously shaped container becomes an architectural monument, the bright fragment of an Art Deco dream."

In 1978 the Los Angeles County Museum of Art presented "Happy's Curios," a masterfully planned installation that took Price four years to produce. Maurice Tuchman, senior curator of modern art at LACMA, correctly described "Happy's Curios" as "a work of art about pottery." And that is precisely Price's own relationship with ceramics. He is making comments about pottery, but as an artist working in several mediums, he does not identify with the title "potter."

The exhibition was billed as a protest, proceeding "from the artist's indignation at the poor state, and low status, of pottery in the art worlds of the U.S. and Europe." It was also described as a homage to the colorful folk pottery of Mexico, a salute to southwestern Indian culture, and several other eulogistic functions. (Price had moved to Taos, New Mexico, in 1971). But in fact the concerns were far broader and far more personal than those declarations of evangelical intent would have us believe. On the one hand it was a most perceptive statement on the thin, shifting line between decorative art and fine art, and on the other a tour de force orchestration of color, surface, and line. The forms (some purchased as blanks from the folk potters themselves) often assumed the role of canvases for his fine draftsmanship and glaze painting.

More successful as a total environment than object by object, nonetheless this was one of the major exhibitions of the decade and a challenge to conventional categories of "art" and "craft." The project was calamitous financially, however; as Price remarked in an interview with Joan Simon, "When I finished . . . I did what we did in Vietnam at the end—I called it a victory and got the hell out."

Since 1978 Price has concentrated on a new body of work that is something of a marriage between his sixties egg forms and early seventies cups. These are vessels to the extent that they deal with volume and suggest spatial containment, but this function is totally abstract, without utilitarian reference. As a result, Price does not intend the pieces to be handled (as he does the cup forms), suggesting that they be viewed as three-dimensional drawings in color.

Color, too, is not decorative as it was in "Happy's Curios," but is used structurally and emotionally. The planar arrangement of brightly glazed surfaces constitutes the content of the work in the same way that color must be dealt with on its own terms in a color field painting. Yet ambiguous references to pottery remain, providing a focus, a sense of scale, and an aesthetic rootedness in an ancient tradition.

Price bisque fires at cone 04 and glaze fires at cone 08 in a gas kiln with an oxidizing atmosphere. The clay body is bone china, composed mainly of talc. The pieces are hand built from thin slabs and are often assembled by an assistant according to Price's drawings. Price uses a wide range of low-fire color glazes.

JERRY ROTHMAN

Jerry Rothman was born in 1933 in Brooklyn, New York, and studied at Los Angeles City College (1953–1955) with the intention of becoming a cabinetmaker. When his interests turned to art, he moved to the Art Center School, Los Angeles (B.A. 1956) and Otis Art Institute, where he worked under Peter Voulkos for two years. He returned to Otis in 1959 to complete his studies (M.F.A. 1961) after a one-year working visit to Japan. Rothman now works from a spacious studio in Laguna Beach, California. From the outset he worked in both pottery and sculpture. In 1957 contact with Edward Kienholz led to an exhibition at the Ferus Gallery in Los Angeles with John Mason, Paul Soldner, and John Altoon. There he showed metal and clay constructions 15 to 20 feet in height.

Rothman's interest in sculpture led to his devising new clay bodies and other innovations, such as cantilevering ceramic sculpture with high-firing metal. His involvement in the vessel ran parallel, first attracting attention in 1960 when he produced a series of *Sky Pots*. These large vessels with their shallow, boxlike shapes stand on pedestallike feet and carry colorful, abstract, sandglazed painting.

Soon thereafter, in the mid-sixties, his pottery began to express a form language that he has consistently explored ever since: freshly erotic forms that are a combination of tightly thrown shapes and exuberant applied decoration, aggressive spouts and handles. Rothman favors a palette of monochrome glazes, opaque whites, and metallic saturate glazes in bronzes, coppers, and golds.

An exhibition at the Vanguard Gallery in 1978 indicated an important step forward in his art. The pottery shows a rhythm, unity, and refinement lacking in previous work. The exhibition title was "Bauhaus-Baroque," a term the artist had coined initially to describe work other than his own. But it became evident that this title summed up the tension or dialectic in his own work between two opposing aesthetics: the one cool, spartan, and classic; the other extravagant, hedonistic, and sensually organic.

Rothman takes pleasure in confounding our preconceptions—about function (his tureens are perfectly utilitarian despite their so-called sculptural look) and good taste, which he rudely and quite deliberately affronts. Good taste usually means "that with which one is comfortable," rather than adherence to any progressive aesthetic standard. To become comfortable with his work requires considerable adjustment in our expectations of the ceramic medium.

Whether one concludes that Rothman's vessels are Bauhaus wolves in baroque clothing or vice versa is unimportant. These strangely disturbing forms with their ambivalence of style challenge the orthodoxy of pottery and in so doing enlarge our definition of both pottery and function.

The pottery is bisque fired at cone 3 and glaze fired at cone 06 in a gas kiln. Most work is fired in a neutral atmosphere, although some pieces are given a second glaze firing in a reduction atmosphere to adjust the color when required. The porcelaneous clay body is covered with metal saturate glazes containing manganese, copper, and iron. A clear frit glaze, which becomes slightly opaque white during oxidation firing, is used occasionally.

PAUL SOLDNER

Paul Soldner was born in Summerfield, Illinois, in 1921. He studied at Bluffton College, Ohio (B.A. 1946), and at the University of Colorado, Boulder (M.A. 1954), where he met Katie Horseman, a visiting lecturer and head of ceramics at Edinburgh College of Art in Scotland. Horseman introduced him to ceramics, and in 1954 Soldner decided to become a potter himself; he was Peter Voulkos's first student at the Los Angeles County Art Institute (M.F.A. 1956). Soldner was one of Voulkos's few students who continued to make functional ceramics at the institute. He did not take a conservative view of his craft, however, but worked on experimental forms such as 6-foot (180 cm) floor pots and other monumental works.

His involvement with raku (a Japanese technique developed in the sixteenth century), for which he is now internationally known, came by chance. Invited to demonstrate at a crafts fair in 1960, Soldner decided to experiment with the technique. Using Bernard Leach's *A Potter's Book* as his guide, he set up a simple kiln and improvised a few lead-based glazes. The results were disappointing: the clay body did not respond well to the quick firing technique, and the glazes were shiny and too brightly colored. His fascination with raku did not diminish, however, and Soldner continued to experiment. At first he produced mainly tea bowls, but soon found these restrictive and somewhat academic, as there was no tea ceremony in Western culture that would give the forms their traditional significance. He gradually discovered he was more interested in raku as a technique and an aesthetic than as a hoary tradition. This attitude resulted in a much more playful approach to form, scale, function, and material.

Soldner traveled extensively, giving lectures and workshops, sharing his discoveries and work. His enthusiasm was infectious; in the process he popularized raku ceramics in the United States. (He later came to understand how very American this technique is in its method and philosophy.) Raku *à la* Soldner became one of the most popular approaches to vessel making in the country, aiding the American potter's search for liberation from European and Oriental domination.

A visit to Japan some ten years after he had began. working in raku proved to be a "shocking discovery" for the potter. Soldner discovered that many of the techniques he thought were traditional were in fact of his own invention. He discovered, too, that raku in Japan is not narrowly defined as a technique, but is more concerned with the transcendental, with rising above technique to achieve a sense of spirituality.

This attitude now dominates Soldner's view of raku. At a recent lecture he remarked that whereas twelve years ago he would have said raku is about the accidental, the spontaneous, today he realizes raku is really about discipline. Soldner equates the word *raku* (meaning "happiness" or "serendipity" in Japanese) with the ease and comfort one sees in the most assured yet casual pottery. In order to achieve such ease, however, the potter must have total command of technique so that he can forget it and surrender to intuition.

Soldner is responsible for creating an entirely new vocabulary of expression in raku and has inspired a generation of Western potters working within that genre, but it is interesting that his own work has a strong sense of continuity with the traditional Japanese view of the medium. In 1972 he offered an explanation of early Japanese raku in *Ceramics Review*; today that description is a fitting definition of his own work: "Traditional Japanese raku incorporates a masterful command of asymmetrical balance in design, a highly developed tactile sensibility in appreciation of materials and a virtuosity of decorative techniques, combined into a unified whole. The overall effect of the work is one of spontaneity achieved in the finished work and characterized by a feeling of an intimate, transitory, insubstantial play of shadows."

Soldner fires in a natural-gas, crossdraft kiln in Claremont, California, and an oil-fired updraft kiln in Aspen, Colorado, at around cone 010 in an oxidation atmosphere. Salt vapors are introduced to change the colors of copper in subsequent firings. Some pieces are complete after the first firing; others are smoked for several hours, after which they are reduced in a bin of paper, wet grass, leaves, and so on. Some are covered with a single clear glaze and white and copper-bearing slips; stains of copper carbonate and iron oxide are also used. The clay body is 30 percent sand, 20 percent talc, 50 percent plastic fire clay.

RUDOLF STAFFEL

Rudolf Staffel was born in San Antonio, Texas, and studied under various artists, including the painters José Arpa and Hans Hofmann in New York. From 1931 he studied at the Art Institute of Chicago, where he worked under Louis Ripman and Laura Van Papelladam. Thereafter he moved to New Orleans, where he taught for the Arts and Crafts Club. From 1940 he taught at the Tyler School of Art, Philadelphia, from which he retired as professor emeritus in 1978.

The breakthrough in Staffel's work dates from his decision to turn to porcelain in the mid-1950s. He had resisted working in this body because he considered it alien to craft traditions. His first works with slip decoration were competent, but it was not until the mid-1960s that his play with the light-transmitting qualities of the material began to produce new forms—a development stemming from his earlier involvement in painting, when light had been his main interest.

Unlike most artists whose works grow less radical with the passage of time, Staffel's porcelain vessels have progressed further and further from the safe conventions of the art. In fact, it would be fair to say that

Staffel is the most radical potter of the group shown here; the forms are asymmetrical, the compositional rhythms contrapuntal, even anarchic at times. In exploiting translucency, Staffel creates a most unusual and dynamic interface between surface and volume.

The works draw their energy from risk. The volatile porcelaneous body he uses requires exact firing temperatures. Failures are frequent, yet Staffel never plays it safe. He has no standard forms; they change from one work period to another. The clay bodies change as well, becoming ever more translucent. "The best body I have worked with," Staffel maintains, "is the body that I know little or nothing about."

The pots are made to have light directed into them, which creates a chiaroscuro effect. Where the porcelain body is thin, the light is intense; as layers of clay are applied or as the walls of the thrown vessels vary in thickness, the amount of light and shade also varies. Color is introduced in some pieces, either through colored clays or with thin metallic washes. The result is a complex, planar surface of rich tonalities, somewhat reminiscent in its virtuoso modulation of light and shade of the better sixteenth-century woodcuts of Ugo da Carpi.

The effect of this is a visual plane that is more than a mere surface. The thinness of the walls—pulsating with light and at times even destroying the corporeality of the clay where light is brightest—creates an intense dialog between inner form (volume) and outer form (mass), for unlike in most pottery, the line dividing the two is ambiguous. The division is suggested partly by the reality of the fired porcelain and partly by the tonal inflections created by the passage of light, which in places invites access to the inner form while in other places denying it.

Staffel fires his work only once in an electric kiln within a temperature range of cone 5 to cone 8 and in an oxidation atmosphere. The body is composed mainly of feldspar and flint, with gums and glues to provide plasticity. Most forms are thrown and then distorted; the greatest challenge in terms of technique is in creating walls of uneven thickness with enough structural strength to survive firing. Color is added either by coloring the body or by painting on the greenware with water-soluble metallic salts such as chloride, sulfate, and nitrate.

SUSANNE STEPHENSON

Susanne Stephenson was born in 1935 in Canton, Ohio, and studied at Carnegie-Mellon University in Pittsburgh and Cranbrook Academy of Art, Bloomfield Hills, Michigan (M.F.A. 1959). Since 1963 Stephenson has taught at Eastern Michigan University, where she is a professor of art. Her work demonstrates a consistent investigation of the vessel form, a pursuit that has taken her to Japan to investigate wood firing and ash glazes (1961–1962) and to Spain to study luster decoration (1973).

In examining the earlier periods of Stephenson's work, one finds an artist searching for a vocabulary. The works are eclectic, the changes in style frequent and often oblique. The past five years, however, have shown Stephenson's true métier; she has emerged somewhat later than her contemporaries but nonetheless has achieved a mature and highly original form of expression.

Stephenson is influenced more by museums of natural history than by museums of art, although she is cognizant of her own history and heritage as a potter. Her pots emerge as complex responses to a variety of inputs: the breakdown of slate walls in canyons, the striations of rock formations, the subtle tonal shading of mesas and desert landscapes, the structure of animal skeletons and skulls. All these aspects are explored in partnership with the clay. As much as any other artist in this book, Stephenson exploits clay's plasticity, its willingness to be formed, manipulated, marked, cut, impressed, textured, and joined. However, her search is less for a doctrinaire "truth to materials" *à la* William Morris than for a quality she describes simply as naturalness, seeking color, surface, and form that seem appropriate at that point in time.

In common with Woodman and others, she feels most at ease with so-called functional forms — lidded jars, plates, bowls, and vases — without expecting the objects to be used. For some time she experimented with forms that had no direct reference to traditional pottery forms but found them lacking in challenge. The excitement of her works comes in part from her acceptance of the limitations that traditional forms seem to imply, then direction of her energies and imagination to finding powerful, contemporary transformations of those forms.

The primary focus of Stephenson's pottery is the rim. Even the frequently energetic bases of the pots, with their structures of extruded elements, seem to take second place. The rims have a surprising abruptness in relationship to the main form; they are roughly faceted, drawn upon, and sometimes combined with thin slabs of clay. The use of color is carefully integrated, dividing the pots into dark and light areas. A wide range of colored slips is used; they are both rubbed into the clay body before firing and applied with a spray gun to achieve careful, soft-focus tonal integration. The vessels are double-walled, creating an interesting disparity between the inner and outer profiles.

Stephenson's porcelain is bisque fired at cone 06 and glaze fired at cone 10. The forms are thrown; the "inner" form is thrown upside down and attached together with extruded elements. Ten to twelve colored slips are applied, both before and after the bisque firing. In the second firing darker-colored slips are applied to make the color relationships more subtle. Two glazes are used: a cone 10 clear glaze and a matte black Albany glaze. The porcelain body is mixed with grog and nylon fiber.

TOSHIKO TAKAEZU

Toshiko Takaezu was born in Pepeekeo, Hawaii, in 1929. She studied with Claude Horan at the Honolulu School of Art and with Maija Grotell at Cranbrook Academy of Art, Bloomfield Hills, Michigan. Takaezu says it was in Hawaii that she learned technique, but it was at Cranbrook that "I found myself." Takaezu readily acknowledges her debt to Grotell in her development as an artist. Grotell's special gift was as a perceptive critic, although Takaezu recalls that the criticism would fall into place only months later: "Maija didn't say very much, and what she didn't say was as important as what she did say, once you realized that she was thoroughly aware of everything that you did."

Takaezu taught for a while at Cranbrook, then directed the ceramics department of the Cleveland Art Institute. In 1968 she gave up full-time teaching (retaining only a part-time involvement with the Creative Arts Program at Princeton University) to devote herself to her work and establish a home and studio in Quakertown, New Jersey.

Over the past three decades Takaezu's work has grown steadily within a particular exploration of form and surface. It reveals a subtle blending of East and West, most readily apparent in the surface treatment. Her vessels with their coverings of dipped, poured, and trickled glazes and slips have the assurance and virtuosity that come from a carefully resolved union of the understatement characteristic of Oriental watercolor landscapes and the aggressive gesture of Abstract Expressionist painting.

Formally, her vessels have always dealt with and been dominated by the sense of enclosure, from her early bird and mask pots to the current work. These pots further underline the constant interplay between masculine and feminine qualities in the vessel. If read in terms of volume (enclosed space), Takaezu's pottery is the female archetype—enclosing, womblike, protective forms. If read in terms of mass (displaced space), however, the pots take on a different quality—masculine, even phallic, in character.

Although Takaezu is concerned with both the vessel's surface and form, she also explores other aspects of pottery. She is keenly interested in the environment of her work in terms of sound, light, and placement. Before closing the minute mouths of her pots, she frequently inserts a piece of fired clay; when the pot is moved, noises are emitted, ranging from the most subtle rustlings to clear, bell-like tones. Takaezu experiments with the presentation of her work as well and now exhibits her *Moon Pots* slung in Honduras string hammocks, while her tall stoneware pillars, up to 70 inches (175 cm) in height, are shown in a forest setting.

A proposed multimedia project involving sophisticated lighting techniques is a clue to one of the central themes of Takaezu's work. In an interview with Joseph Hurley, Takaezu outlined her plans, which call for the light diminishing as the viewer approaches her pottery. "It's almost like one human being getting to know another," she remarked, "because when you get close to an individual you find you really know him. I think it is very difficult to get to know what any person is truly like. That's how I feel about human relationships, not that they close up exactly, although I have thought of making a pot with a suspended lid which closes as you come near it." Her work is finally an exploration of the privacy of space—space that in her pots is as much guarded as it is enclosed. It is the penetration of those defenses that is the key to getting to know the gentle power of Takaezu's pottery.

Takaezu fires in a two-chamber, downdraft, propane-fueled kiln. The wares are bisque fired between cone 06 and 09 in the upper bisque chamber of the kiln, while the glaze firing takes place in the lower chamber between cone 9 and 10. Takaezu uses two clay bodies, one porcelain, the other stoneware, which she mixes according to her requirements. She uses mostly ash glazes and a plain white glaze with copper and other oxides. The glazes are variously brushed, dipped, poured, and sprayed on her forms. Apart from the tile pieces, all forms are wheel thrown.

Robert Turner

Robert Turner was born in Port Washington, New York, in 1913. He studied at Swarthmore College, Pennsylvania (B.A. 1936), and for the following five years studied painting at the Pennsylvania Academy of Art, Philadelphia, and the Barnes Foundation, Merion, Pennsylvania. He also spent some years in Europe painting and studying at public museums. Upon his return to the United States, however, Turner found that his interest in painting was being displaced by pottery. After a period of internment as a conscientious objector during World War Two, Turner entered the New York State College of Clayworking and Ceramics at Alfred University, remaining there from 1946 to 1949. That period was an important transitional time for both Turner and the college; the latter was then beginning to shed its designerly approach to ceramics for a more vigorous one. While at Alfred, Turner worked with Daniel Rhodes; other fellow students destined to play a role in the growth of ceramics during the 1950s included Minnie Negero, Ted Randall, David Weinrib, and David Gil.

After leaving Alfred University, Turner moved to Black Mountain College in North Carolina. He built and established a pottery there, which he handed over in 1951 to two Alfred graduates, Weinrib and Karen Karnes. He returned to Alfred Station and in the following year built a studio and home on a 100-acre farm, where he still lives today. There he divided his time between his pottery and teaching at Alfred.

Except for a period of dabbling with earthenware during his student years, Turner was drawn to the qualities of stoneware from the outset and has worked in this body throughout his career. He was inspired in the 1940s by English potter and Surrealist painter Sam Haile, Alex Giampietro, and other visitors to Alfred. Despite his training as a painter, Turner was never drawn to painting his vessels. He occasionally uses a few lines or circles of slip, or some sgraffito, but his primary interest is form.

In Turner's pottery, as in the work of many other potters described in this book, one senses that dialectic between inner and outer form. In Turner's case the tensions created are perhaps less stressful; there is a softness, a languorous sensuality, to the forms. The tease between negative and positive is neither cerebral nor structured in a self-conscious sense, but suggests a continuous caress, a soft probing of negative and positive space. Above all, Turner's forms provide a sense of inner volume, a quality seen in the finest pottery of the past: the swelling reality of a form that grows naturally from the volume contained within.

The influences in Turner's work are various. At one stage Chinese stoneware inspired him. But in the seventies the work of Peter Voulkos on the one hand and a deep empathy for West Africa and traditional West African form on the other began to alter his work radically. The defining lines in his vessels began to soften, the rims became irregular, square necks appeared in round forms, and domed lids gave a new monumentality to his lidded vessels. Color was reduced to a palette of cinnamon, charcoal, and white.

His primary inspiration is the landscape, the desert, and the sea. In 1963 he wrote that "the natural processes with clays and glazes are appropriate when one is interested in the expression of enduring values as seen in natural objects." At the time he sought what he termed "the surprise of contrast" that he found in seashells. More recently he spoke of drawing on his pots (varied techniques of impressing, texturing, imprinting, and applying relief sections), likening the process to that of the traces left on the seashore by the play of waves and tides.

For many, Turner is the doyen of the traditionalists. His forms acknowledge pottery as an art of limitations, seeking an expressive essence through repetition and reinterpretation of a limited and established form vocabulary. One can compare the process to that of a gifted classical musician who constantly works for a purer and purer performance of a known composition.

Turner bisque fires his natural-gas kiln at cone 08 to 010 and glaze fires at cone 9 in a reduction atmosphere. A cinnamon glaze of dolomite, tin, and bone ash and a charcoal glaze of cobalt, chrome, and dolomite over Albany slip are used on the stoneware forms; a white Leach-type glaze of feldspar, flint, whiting, and clay is used on the porcelain forms. Surfaces are sandblasted so the pots "absorb light rather than reflect it, soften the otherwise austere forms and draw the viewer closer."

PETER VOULKOS

Peter Voulkos was born in Bozeman, Montana, in 1924. He studied painting at Montana State University (B.S. 1949) and ceramics at California College of Arts and Crafts (M.F.A. 1952). In 1951 he began to work at the Archie Bray Foundation with resident sculptor Rudy Autio.

The crucial change in his work came in 1954, when he was appointed chairman of the ceramics department at Otis Art Institute, Los Angeles. Several factors contributed to this break: his involvement in progressive jazz and studying the classical guitar; the ceramics of Picasso, Miró, Chagall, Fontana, and others; and the folk potters of Japan—Hamada, Kawai, Rosanjin, Kaneshige. Equally important were the students who gathered around Voulkos, forming a highly synergistic, competitive working environment. Last, and perhaps the most overstated influence, was Abstract Expressionism, for his new style was already established before Rose Slivka introduced him to the luminaries of the New York School in the late fifties. Much inspiration came from Voulkos's voracious appetite for historical ceramics, which he satisfied mainly through books. Voulkos discovered only later that the "huge" works illustrated, which had inspired him to work in large scale, were in fact rather small. Picasso was another formative influence, as many of Voulkos's plates made from 1954 to 1958 demonstrate. A freewheeling empiricism, however, is what finally forges all these ingredients into a unique alloy that is his alone. Voulkos himself concisely summed up his working philosophy in an interview with Conrad Brown (*Craft Horizons*, October 1956): "The minute you begin to feel you understand what you are doing [you] lose that searching quality. . . . You finally reach a point where you're no longer concerned with keeping this blob of clay centered on the wheel and up in the air. . . . Your emotions take over and what happens, happens."

From 1954 to 1961 Voulkos created thousands of pots, constantly surpassing the boundaries of what had been considered acceptable form in Western ceramics. In 1958 he joined the faculty of the University of California at Berkeley, where his interests shifted toward sculpture. In 1961 Voulkos announced his withdrawal from the ceramic world. Despite this pronouncement, he continued to work sporadically in ceramics (the 1966 exhibition at Quay Gallery was particularly memorable) and frequently lectured and demonstrated. In 1973 he produced a series of two hundred plates (thrown by an assistant) covered with brusquely drawn lines, punctured surfaces, and pellets of porcelain inserted into the stoneware body. His most stylish and elegant body of work, it was disappointing formally, recalling Voulkos's admonition twenty-four years earlier that he would "rather pump gas" than decorate other people's pottery. A second series followed, this time with Voulkos himself at the wheel, and the forms were much stronger as a result.

Voulkos occasionally produces tall pottery forms, refined from the shapes he introduced in 1966, but the carefree experimentation is gone, replaced by more consciously structured compositions.

Until recently his plates were fired in a gas kiln with a thin covering of commercial glaze that produced a pseudo-wood-fired appearance. In the past couple of years Voulkos has been firing in a single-chambered wood kiln, which has returned an element of the unexpected to his work. Once the product of his impetuous talent, this unpredictability now derives from the kiln, which covers the surface in surprising color, tone, and movement that complement his powerful surface drawings.

The plates shown here, except for one fired in Voulkos's gas kiln in Oakland, were all reduction fired at cone 10 to 11 in a Japanese anagama *wood kiln. The sheen of the unglazed surfaces comes from the ash flashing and the action of the fire. Dark black and blue markings are encouraged by stacking wood against the plates. The gas-fired plate was bisque fired at cone 1 and refired in a reduction atmosphere at cone 5.*

BEATRICE WOOD

Beatrice Wood was born in 1894 in San Francisco. While in her late teens she studied in Paris at that mecca for the American art student, Académie Julian. She found the stage more attractive, however, and transferred to the Académie Française. Upon her return to the United States she joined the French Repertory Company in New York City.

It was in New York, while visiting the French composer Edgard Varèse in the hospital, that she was introduced to Marcel Duchamp. She became an intimate friend of the artist and a member of his recherché cultural clique that included Francis Picabia, Man Ray, Albert Gleizes, Henri Pierre Roché, and others. Soon Wood became active in the group and contributed articles and drawings to Duchamp's avant-garde magazines, *Rogue* and *Blind Man*.

It was not until she was in her forties, in 1938, that she became interested in ceramics. Wood had acquired a set of luster cups from an antique dealer in Holland and decided that she had to have a teapot as well. Upon her return to California, having been unable to find the teapot she sought, she decided to make one herself and was offered studio facilities at the Hollywood High School. She recalls thinking that one weekend would be enough to produce a teapot; in fact, several weeks resulted in little more than a few barely serviceable plates.

Intrigued, Wood set up a studio in North Hollywood, studying with Glen Lukens at the University of Southern California, Los Angeles, and briefly

with Gertrud and Otto Natzler. Wood then moved to Ojai, a tranquil town about sixty miles north, where she built a studio and home. She later sold this to potters Vivika and Otto Heino and moved to the Happy Valley Foundation, just outside the town, with which she had been closely involved since its establishment as a theosophical school in 1946 by Aldous Huxley, Krishnamurti, and Annie Besant.

There Wood has developed a uniquely expressive art form with her lusterwares. These works reveal that her sense of theater is still alive in the play with vivid, glimmering surfaces and informal, lively forms. Wood's lusterwares instruct us that working with luster is not for the timid. It can be an overwhelming and fickle technique (much like crystalline glazing) that seems to succeed only at one extreme or the other—absolute understatement or total ebullience. Wood has opted for the latter, saturating her goblets, vases, and teapots in shining viridian greens, peacock blues, crimsons, and golds.

One finds the same fearless approach to color and light in her lusterware as in that of the earlier modern masters of the technique: France's Clement Massier, England's William De Morgan, and Italy's Pietro Melandri. In searching for the fullest, most unfettered effect of luster, however, the artist treads a very thin line between panache and vulgarity. The delicacy of Wood's forms, a certain naiveté in the clay handling, and the witty use of color save her from the negative excesses of the technique.

The scintillating magic that she conjures in her pottery occurs only occasionally, as Wood is the first to admit. Often an entire firing produces only one successful piece; at times no fine pieces are produced at all.

This unevenness is not a matter of critical concern. Wood's style is one of constant change and experiment, and failures are, after all, the by-products of risk taking. Finally, as with all artists, Wood must be judged by her masterworks, and certainly these are sufficient in number to earn her a very special place in American pottery, a place she has achieved by following the artistic credo given her by Duchamp: "Never do the commonplace; rules are fatal to the progress of art."

Wood uses an electric kiln, firing in both oxidation and reduction atmospheres. The pots are bisque fired at cone 08 and glaze fired around cone 04 to 08. Wood is secretive about her inglaze lusters, remarking that they are "as much a secret to me." Her glazes, arrived at by highly empirical experiments, are unpredictable and results can rarely be exactly reproduced. Wood uses a local red earthenware clay body and throws all her forms on an electric wheel.

BETTY WOODMAN

Betty Woodman was born in Norwalk, Connecticut, in 1930 and studied pottery at the School for American Craftsmen at Alfred University, Alfred, New York, from 1948 to 1950. She set up a studio soon after completing her studies, and ceramics has remained her major source of income ever since. For a time she was involved in an adult education program in Boulder, Colorado, where she lives. In 1976 she joined the faculty of the University of Colorado, Boulder, as an assistant professor, and she teaches there one semester a year. Woodman now maintains three studios: in Boulder, Colorado; New York City; and Florence, Italy.

Woodman is one of the artists responsible for the recent revival of interest in earthenware. This involvement began in 1973 in Italy, where Woodman and her husband, painter George Woodman, spend their summers in a farmhouse outside Florence. There she became interested in the peculiarities of lead glazes, the soft, nonvitreous clays, and the possibility of "bright colors and lively decorations that move only slightly in the firing."

Her work reflects a strong interest in and commitment to the traditions of pottery. She uses a palette of color that was originated during the T'ang dynasty (the "three color" glazes) and then spread through Persia to Spain, Italy, and Mexico. "I find it fascinating," she stated in the catalog of her 1980

one-woman exhibition at the Rochester Art Center, "that much of the world's ceramics have evolved from one culture's attempt to imitate another. . . . My formal ideas start that way in observation and interpretation of certain qualities in objects from other cultures and times."

Certainly, Woodman captures this cultural connection in her work, which combines the looseness and abstraction of T'ang decoration with the voluptuousness of full-bodied Mediterranean forms. These qualities coalesce with the larger-than-usual scale and bravura clay handling that are identifiably American in spirit.

No matter the source of her inspiration; Woodman's prime commitment is to the nature of clay itself. This is true for many potters, but for Woodman it is the overwhelming consideration. The forms she selects, the surfaces and structures, are all chosen to exploit fully clay's plasticity and to keep the first wet, soft forms alive in the "memory" of the fired pot. This hard-soft dichotomy is one with which we are familiar in post–World War II art, Claes Oldenburg's soft sculptures being the most obvious example.

In pursuit of this freshness of surface and form, Woodman has become one of the most facile manipulators of clay in America, building with thrown elements, forming handles, and adding surface ornament with seeming effortlessness and great speed. The accent in her forms is upon assembly and structure. Many of the more complex assemblies have an almost architectural quality. In this regard Woodman's handles are of particular interest. These large, curving clay elements bind the forms together while standing as powerful decorative statements in themselves, overstated at times to the point of parody.

Woodman's pottery is bisque fired in a gas kiln at cone 08 and glaze fired at cone 05 in an oxidation atmosphere. The pottery made in Italy is once fired in a kerosene-burning kiln in a reduction atmosphere. The terra sigillata pieces are also once fired. Two clay bodies are used: a white earthenware composed of equal parts of ball clay, kaolin, and fire clay (with fluxes) and a red clay composed of equal parts of Redart clay, ball clay, fire clay with some fluxes added, and occasionally sand. A clear lead glaze is used, which is then painted with onglaze colors. The pottery is thrown in sections and assembled. Most of the handles and other elements are cut out of large thrown cylinders.

RUDY AUTIO

◄TWO LADIES AND DOG
(1979), 29" (73.7 cm) high,
stoneware.

►TWO LADIES: TWO DOGS
(1979), 25" (63.5 cm) high,
stoneware.

56

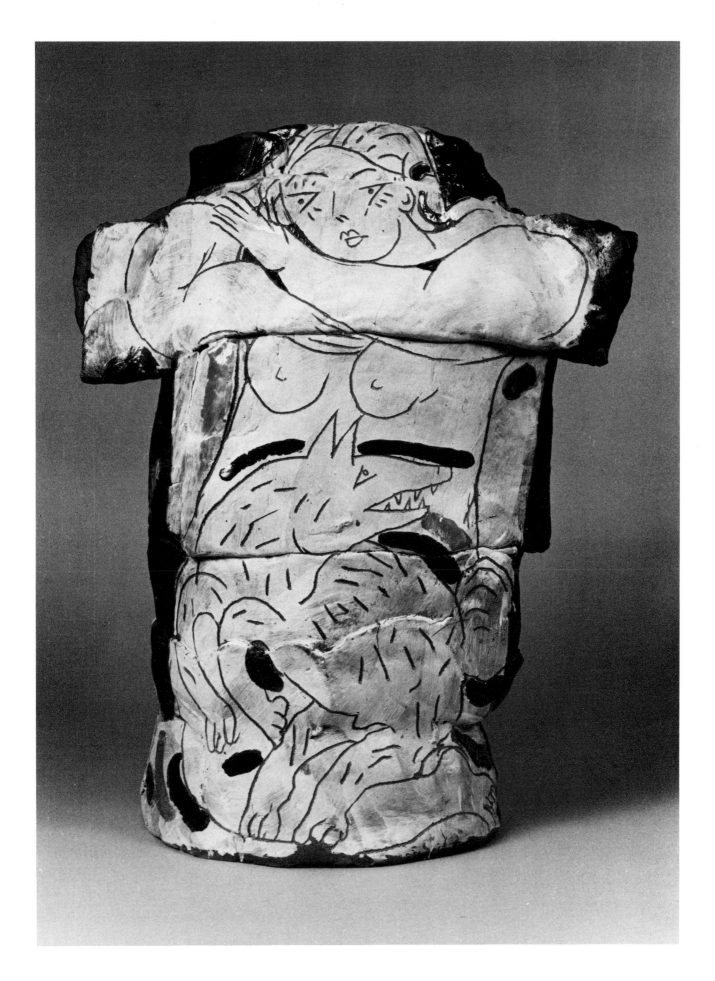

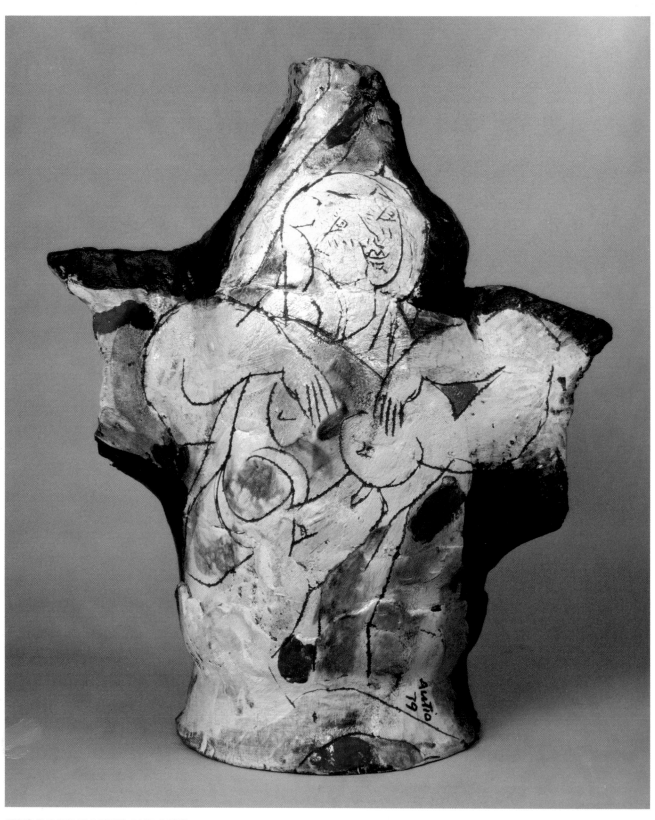

TWO FLOATING LADIES AND COW
(1979), 30″ (76.2 cm) high, stoneware.

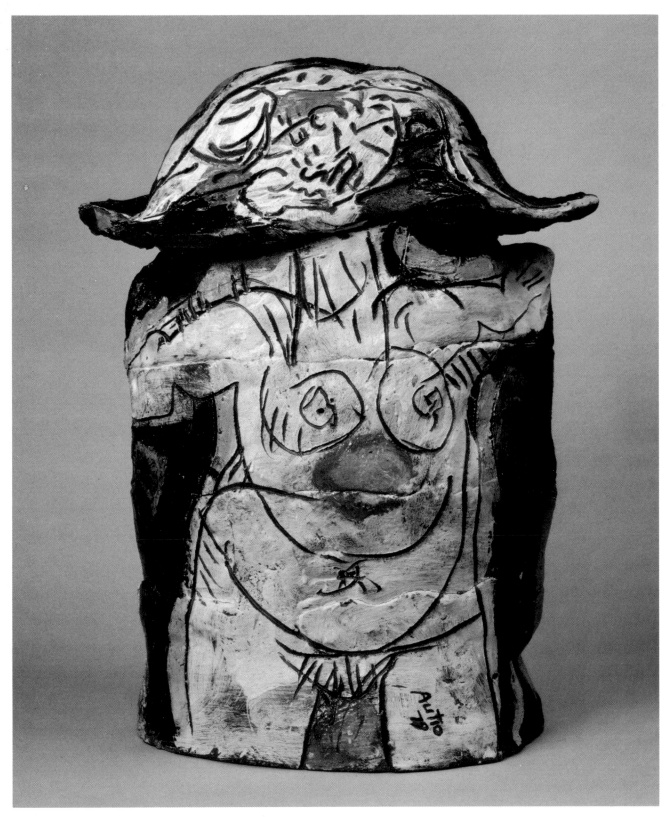

THREE LADIES
(1979), 29″ (73.7 cm) high, stoneware.

VAL CUSHING

▲ROUND APPLE JAR
(1980), 16½″ (41.9 cm) high, stoneware.

▶STRAIGHT APPLE JAR
(1980), 21″ (53.3 cm) high, stoneware.

STRAIGHT APPLE JAR
(1980), 20″ (50.8 cm) high, stoneware.

ACORN ROLL TOP JAR
(1980), 17″ (43.2 cm) high, stoneware.

WILLIAM DALEY

AXIAL INN
(1980), 12½″ × 18″ × 22″ (31.8 × 45.7 × 55.9 cm), stoneware. Courtesy Helen Drutt Gallery, Philadelphia. Two views.

KIVA SQUARED
(1980), 11½" (29.2 cm) high × 25" (63.5 cm)
in diameter, stoneware. Courtesy Helen Drutt
Gallery, Philadelphia. Two views.

▲UNTITLED
(1979), 11″ × 22″ × 23″ (27.9 × 55.9 × 58.3 cm), stoneware.
Courtesy Braunstein Gallery, San Francisco.

▶UNTITLED
(1978), 11″ × 17″ × 19″ (27.9 × 43.2 × 48.3 cm), stoneware.
Courtesy Helen Drutt Gallery, Phildelphia. Two views.

Richard DeVore

▲ UNTITLED
(1980), 15½″ (39.4 cm) high, stoneware. Courtesy Exhibit A,
Chicago.

► UNTITLED
(1980), 12″ (30.5 cm) high, stoneware. Courtesy Exhibit A,
Chicago.

◄UNTITLED
(1979), 13″ (33 cm) high, stoneware.
Courtesy Exhibit A, Chicago.

►UNTITLED
(1980), 4″ × 6½″ × 6¼″ (10.2 × 16.5
× 16 cm), stoneware. Courtesy Exhibit A,
Chicago.

►UNTITLED
(1980), 3″ × 7½″ (7.6 × 19 cm),
stoneware. Courtesy Exhibit A, Chicago.

KENNETH FERGUSON

◄ADAM AND EVE
(1980), 17″ (43.2 cm) in diameter,
porcelain. Private collection.

◄ADAM AND EVE
(1980), 19½″ (49.6 cm) in diameter,
porcelain.

▶BASKET
(1980), 12″ (30.5 cm) high,
stoneware.

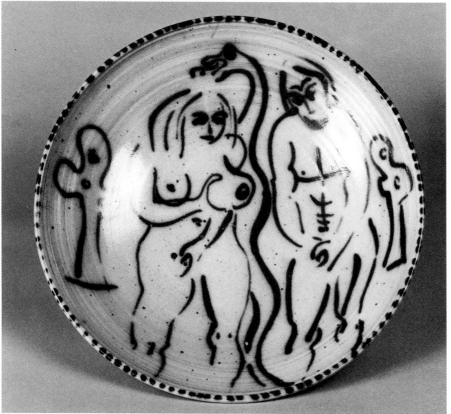

▲PLATTER
(1980), 18″ (45.7 cm) in diameter, porcelain. Private collection.

◄TEAPOT
(1979), 13″ (33 cm) high, stoneware. Private collection.

MICHAEL FRIMKESS

◄THE MARRIAGE OF AUNTIE SUSANNA
(1977), 31¾″ (80.6 cm) high, earthenware.

►CASA GLORIA
(1977–78), 28½″ (72.4 cm) high, stoneware.
Two views.

▲ECOLOGY KRATER II
(1976), 26″ (66 cm) high, stoneware.
Collection Daniel Jacobs.

▶TEMPLE VASE
(1977–78), 25″ (63.5 cm) high, stoneware.

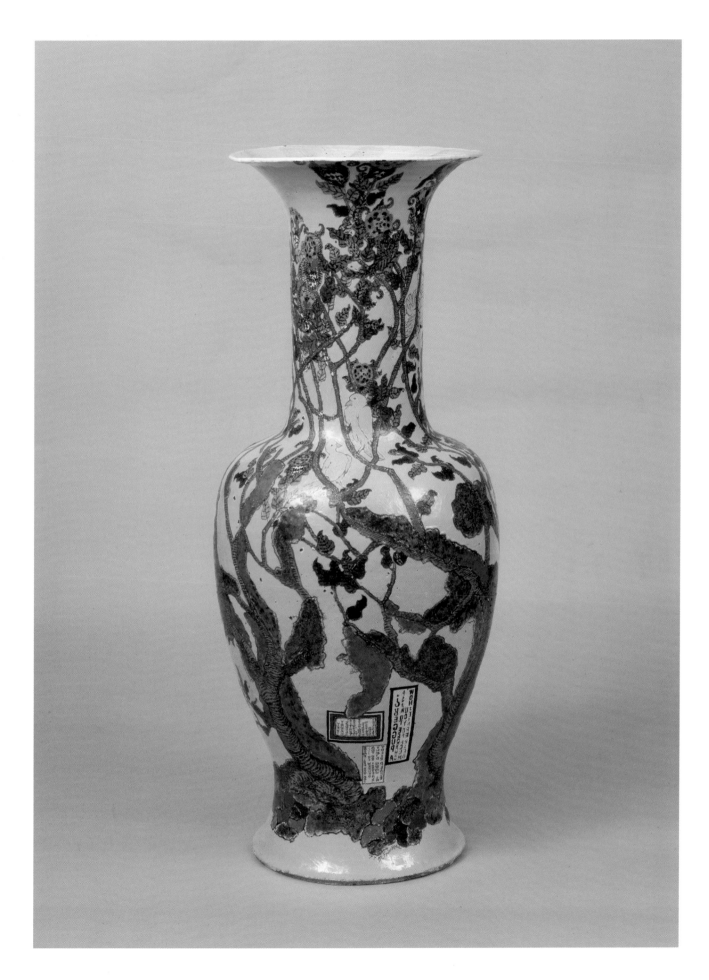

JOHN GLICK

▲PLATE
(1979), 11½″ (29.2 cm) in diameter, porcelain. Courtesy
Helen Drutt Gallery, Philadelphia.

◄BOX
(1977), 3½″ × 5″ × 7″ (9 × 13 × 18 cm), stoneware.
Private collection.

▶TEAPOT
(1979), 9¼″ (23.5 cm) high,
stoneware.

▼BOWL
(1979), 16″ (40.6 cm) in
diameter, stoneware.

PLATE
(1978), 13⅜″ (34 cm) in
diameter, stoneware.

KAREN KARNES

◀BOWL
(1980), 14½″ (36.8 cm) in
diameter, stoneware.
Courtesy Hadler/Rodriguez
Galleries, New York.

▶COVERED JAR
(1980), 18½″ (47 cm) high,
stoneware. Courtesy
Hadler/Rodriguez Galleries,
New York.

COVERED JAR
(1979), 8" (20.3 cm) high, porcelain.

COVERED JAR
(1979), 7" (17.8 cm) high, stoneware.

WARREN MACKENZIE

▶BOWL
(1979), 20¾" (52.7 cm)
in diameter, stoneware.

▲TEAPOT
(1980), 4½" (11.5 cm) high without handle, stoneware.

▶TRIPOD PLATE
(1979), 13⅝" (34.6 cm) in diameter, porcelain.

▲<u>COVERED JAR</u>
(1979), 7″ (17.8 cm) high, stoneware.

▶<u>VASE</u>
(1979), 11″ (27.9 cm) high, stoneware.

RON NAGLE

UNTITLED CUP
(1979), 3" (7.6 cm) high, earthenware. Private
collection.

STUCCOYAMA NO. 1
(1978), 4" (10.2 cm) high, earthenware.
Courtesy Quay Gallery, San Francisco.

VERDEYAMA
(1978), 3¼″ (8.2 cm) high, earthenware.
Courtesy Quay Gallery, San Francisco.

EXPRESSO YAMA NO. 1
(1978), 4¼″ (10.8 cm) high, earthenware.
Courtesy Quay Gallery, San Francisco.

MINI MORANOYAMA
(1980) 2″ (5.1 cm) high, earthenware. Courtesy
Quay Gallery, San Francisco.

UNTITLED (MINIYAMA SERIES)
(1980), 2¾″ (7 cm) high, earthenware. Courtesy
Quay Gallery, San Francisco.

UNTITLED CUP
(1980), 3½″ (8.9 cm) high, earthenware. Courtesy
Quay Gallery, San Francisco.

SKINNY MINIYAMA
(1980), 2⅞″ (7.3 cm) high, earthenware. Courtesy
Quay Gallery, San Francisco.

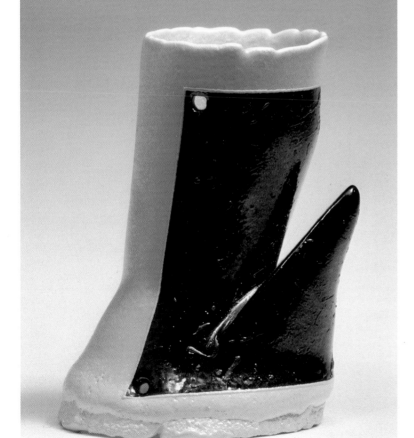

KENNETH PRICE

UNTITLED (THE WEDGE)
(1980), 5⅝" (14.3 cm) high, bone china.

AVOCADO AND WINE
(1980), 6⅝" (16.8 cm) high, bone china. Private collection.

PITTSBURGH
(1979), 9⅛" (23.2 cm) high, bone china.
Courtesy Willard Gallery, New York.

CIRCUS RING
(1979—80), 5″ (12.7 cm) high, bone china.

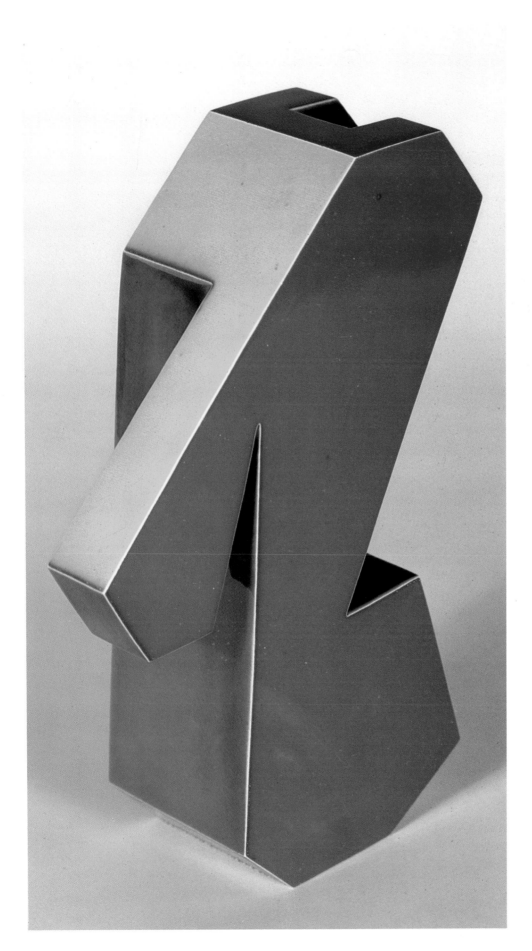

FLAG
(1980), 9⅜″ (23.9 cm) high,
bone china. Private
collection.

JERRY ROTHMAN

◄RITUAL VESSEL
(1980), 22″ (55.9 cm) high,
porcelain.

►BICENTENNIAL TUREEN
(1976), 20″ (50.8 cm) high,
porcelain.

▲TUREEN
(1979), 17⅛″ (43.5 cm) high, porcelain.

►COFFEE POT
(1978), 17½″ (44.4 cm) high, porcelain.

PAUL SOLDNER

◄VOCO
(1979), 21½" (54.5 cm) high, raku.

►VOCO
(1979), 17½" (44.4 cm) high, raku.

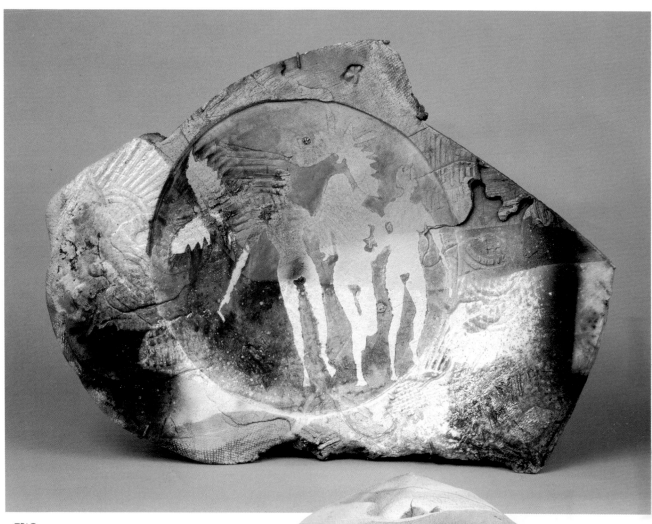

▲TRIO
(1977), 17¾" (45.1 cm) high, raku.

◄VOCO
(1978), 18" (46 cm) high, raku.

►VOCO
(1978), 11" (27.9 cm) high, raku.
Collection Lynne Wagner.

RUDOLF STAFFEL

▲ LIGHT GATHERER
(1976), 5½″ × 11¾″ × 10¾″ (14 × 29.8 × 27.3 cm),
porcelain. Courtesy Helen Drutt Gallery, Philadelphia.

▶ LIGHT GATHERER
(ca. 1972), 5″ (12.7 cm) high × 5¾″ (14.6 cm) in diameter,
porcelain. Courtesy Helen Drutt Gallery, Philadelphia.

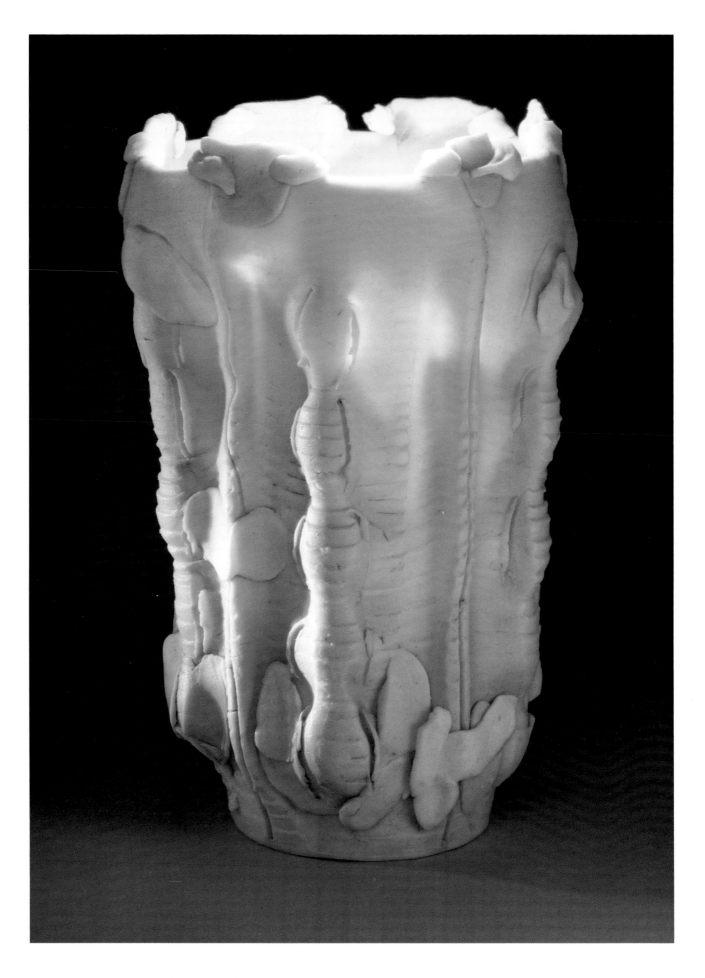

◄LIGHT GATHERER
(1976), 9″ (22.9 cm) high × 5″
(12.7 cm) in diameter, porcelain.
Courtesy Helen Drutt Gallery,
Philadelphia.

►LIGHT GATHERER
(1978), 11″ (27.9 cm) high,
porcelain. Private collection.

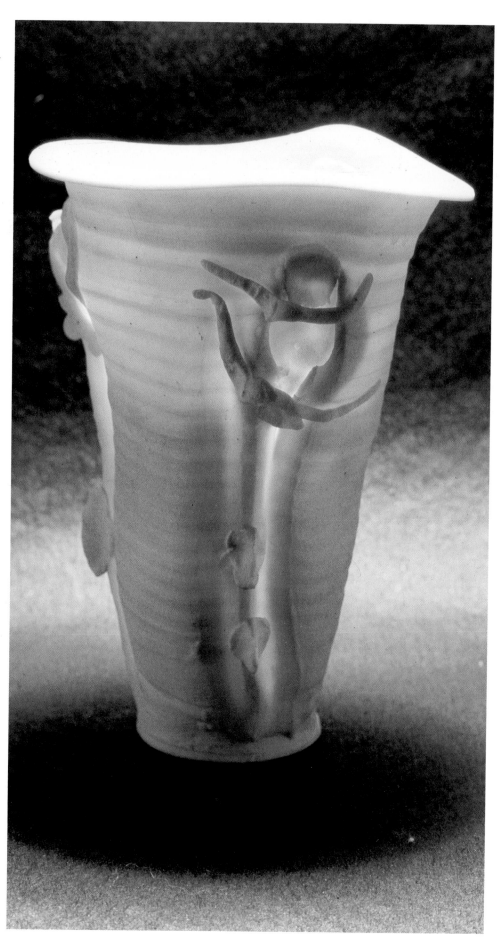

SUSANNE STEPHENSON

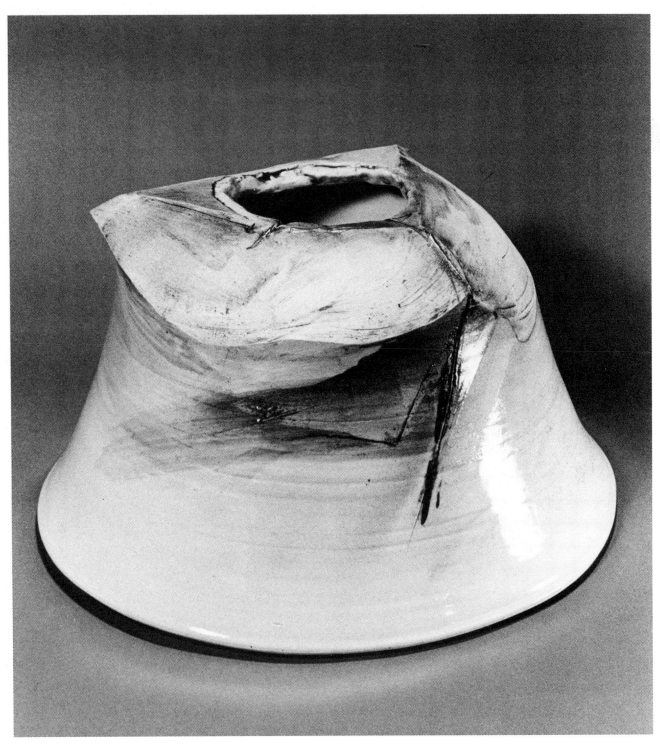

CUT EDGE VASE
(1980), 10″ (25.4 cm) high, porcelain.

CUT EDGE FORM
(1979), 12″ (30.5 cm) high, porcelain.

▲UNTITLED
(1979), 12″ (30.5 cm) high, porcelain.

◀UNTITLED
(1978), 17″ (43.2 cm) high, porcelain.

TOSHIKO TAKAEZU

◄YORU
(1979), 8⅜″ (21.3 cm) high, stoneware.

▼U-GATA
(1979), 10⅞″ (27.6 cm) in diameter, porcelain.

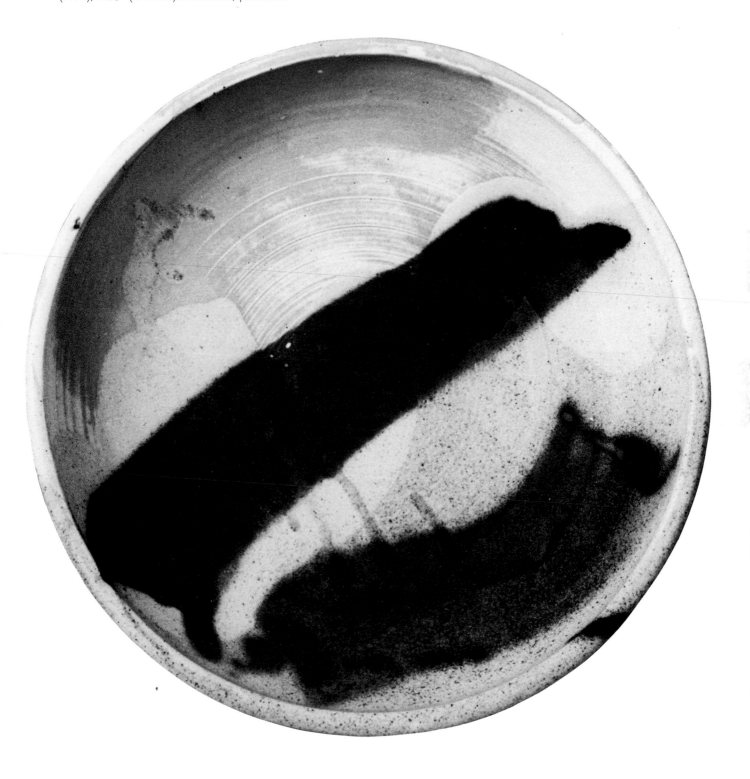

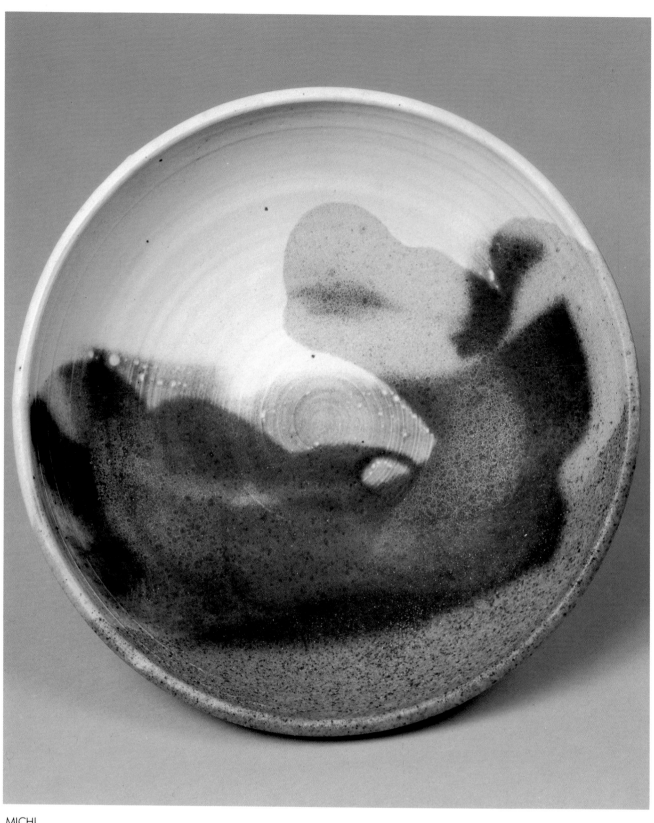

MICHI
(1979), 14½″ (36.9 cm) in diameter, porcelain.

MURASAKI
(1979), 7⅜″ (18.8 cm) high, porcelain.

ROBERT TURNER

◀UNTITLED
(1977), 14" (35.6 cm) high, stoneware.

▼UNTITLED
(1977), 10" (25.4 cm) high, stoneware.

▶AKAN VI
(1980), 10" (25.4 cm) high, porcelain. Courtesy Helen
Drutt Gallery, Philadelphia.

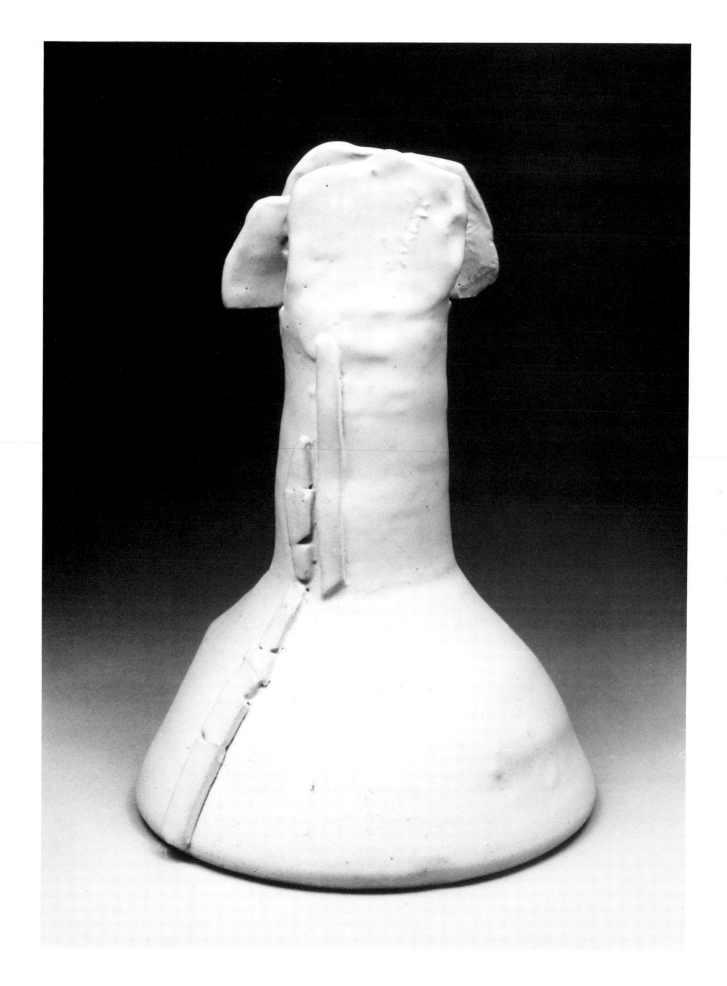

AKAN II
(1979), 14¼″ (36.2 cm) high, stoneware.

DOME I
(1979), 10½" (26.8 cm) high, stoneware.
Courtesy Exhibit A, Chicago.

PETER VOULKOS

UNITLED
(1980), 17½″ (44.5 cm) in diameter, stoneware.

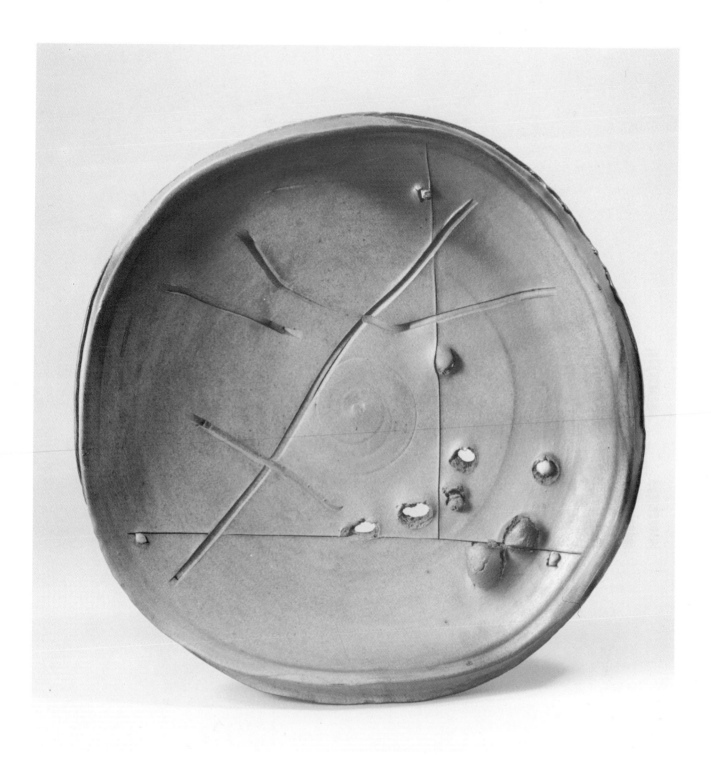

UNTITLED
(1980), 18½" (47 cm) in diameter, stoneware.

UNTITLED
(1979), 18″ × 19″ (45.7 × 48.3 cm), stoneware.

UNDERLINE
UNTITLED
(1980), 19″ × 18½″ (48.3 × 47 cm), stoneware.

◄GOBLET
(1976), 9½″ (24.3 cm) high, earthenware.

►BOTTLE
(1980), 6″ (15.2 cm) high, earthenware.

►GOBLET
(1980), 9″ (23 cm) high, earthenware.

BOTTLE
(1978-79), 7¾" (19.7 cm) high, earthenware.

BOTTLE
(1978), 6¼″ (15.8 cm) high, earthenware.

BETTY WOODMAN

◄MERINGUE VASE
(1979), 6″ × 5″ × 10″ (15.2 × 12.7 × 25.4 cm), white earthenware. Collection Ree Schonlau.

►VINE VASE
(1980), 12½″ (31.8 cm) high, white earthenware.

▼OVAL BASKET WITH CONSOLE HANDLES
(1979), 6″ × 11″ × 32″ (15.2 × 27.9 × 81.3 cm), white earthenware.

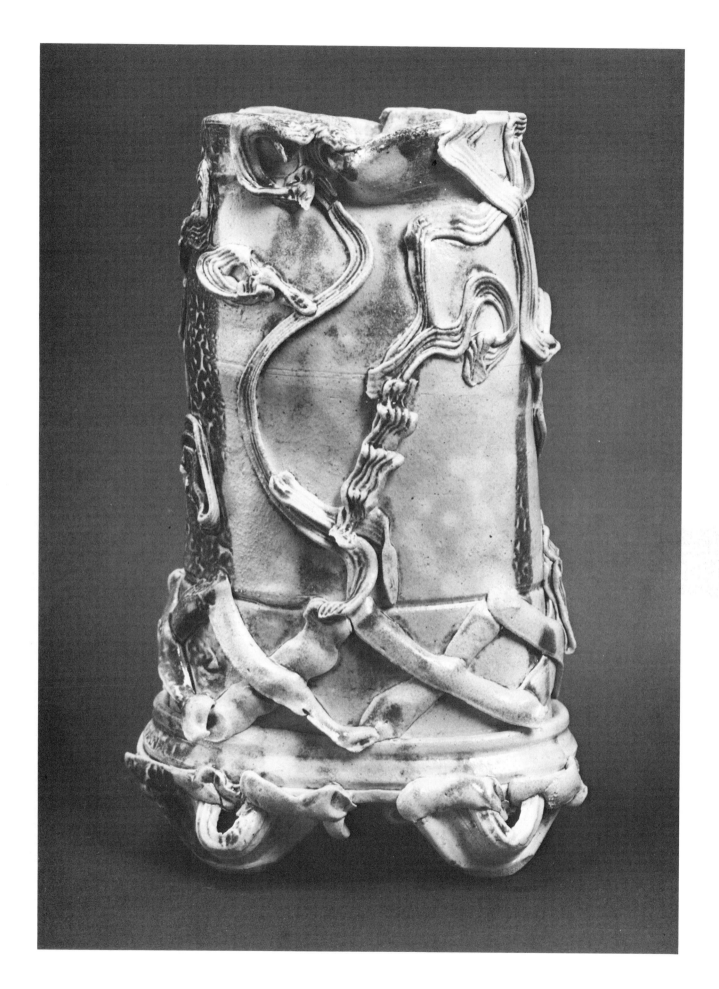

BOUDOIR BASKET
(1980), 9″ × 10½″ × 13″ (22.9 × 26.7 × 33 cm), white earthenware.

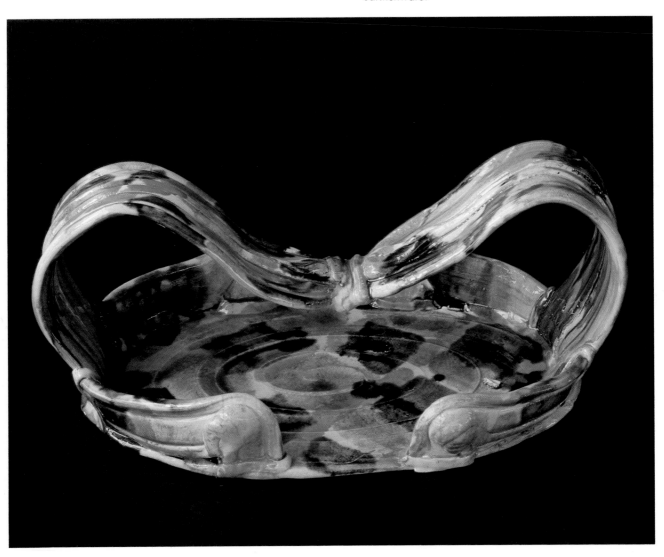

▶MINOAN PILLOW PITCHER
(1979), 13¾″ (34.9 cm) high × 24″ (61 cm)
long, earthenware.

▼"T'ANG" PILLOW PITCHER
(1980), 18″ (45.7 cm) high × 26″ (66 cm) long,
white earthenware.

GLOSSARY

Applied decoration. A decoration created by applying pieces of clay to the surface of the form.

Ball clay. A fine-grained, plastic clay used in clay bodies to increase plasticity.

Bisque firing. A first firing that prepares the ceramic surface to receive the glaze, after which it is refired.

Bizen. A Japanese ware known for its intentional uneven firing and chance effects.

Body. The trunk or main portion of a vessel. In the phrase "clay body," it indicates the composition of a particular clay blended for a specific purpose.

Celadon. A glaze type ranging from green to green-gray developed by the Chinese to imitate the color and qualities of jade.

China clay (kaolin). A refractory white clay required to make true or feldspathic porcelain. It is also used to blend clay bodies and as an ingredient in high-fired glazes. China clay is formed by the decomposition of granite.

China paint. An onglaze enamel produced from finely ground low-firing glass. This is painted, airbrushed, or otherwise applied to the already glazed and fired surface of a pot, which is then refired at around 700° C. China painting provides an infinite range of color; however, its use by the potter and sculptor is recent, having been looked down upon as a hobbyist's material until the early 1960s. Ron Nagle was one of the first to develop the use of china paint, returning this technique to artistic respectability.

Crackle (craquelle). A deliberate technique of creating a glaze surface covered in fine fissures.

Crawling. The result of poor "fit" between clay and glaze, or as the turn-of-the-century ceramics scholar William Burton described it, "a want of agreement." The glaze tends to break from the body and "crawl" into pools.

Crazing. A fine cracking on the glaze surface.

Earthenware. A low-fired (under 1,100° C) clay body. Earthenware is porous and must be glazed if the vessel is to hold water. Raku, majolica, faience, delftware, Egyptian paste, and creamware are all earthenware. Earthenware was a popular body among American studio potters until the Second World War, when the higher-fired bodies, stoneware and porcelain, gained favor. There is now a revival of interest in earthenware in which Betty Woodman has played a major and controversial role.

Engobe. A synonym for *slip*, although it generally means that colors (oxides) have been added to the clay.

Fire clay. A refractory clay—a clay that is resistant to high temperatures—which can be fired to temperatures of up to 1,650° C. and is mostly used for fire bricks and kiln furniture. Some potters who produce large forms (Rudy Autio, for instance) blend quantities of fire clay to prevent warping and cracking.

Flashing. A marking or coloration mostly associated with wood firings that occurs when fine ash particles settle on the pot surface. Techniques exist to encourage this "happenstance," such as painting the inside of saggers with volatile materials.

Flux. An agent added to glazes (and some clays) to reduce the temperature necessary for the fusion of the glaze.

Frit. A prefired and finely ground ingredient in glazes.

Glaze. A nonporous covering of glass that is fused to the clay body during firing.

***Grand feu* ceramics** (Fr. "great fire"). A term that became popular at the turn of the century to describe ceramics fired to stoneware and porcelain temperatures.

Greenware. Wares that have already been formed and, although no longer plastic, are not yet dry enough to be fired.

Grog. A roughly ground prefired material used to strengthen clay bodies.

Impressed decoration. The stamping of motifs directly into the plastic surface of the clay, using a tool of some kind.

Inglaze. A color or decoration placed on an unfired glaze with which it then fuses during firing. The tin-glazed majolica of the Renaissance is a fine example of this form of decoration. It requires sureness and accuracy on the part of the decorator, as errors cannot be amended or painted out.

Kaki glaze. A rust-colored glaze, Japanese in origin, named after the persimmon fruit, frequently used to complement Tenmoku glaze.

Kaolin. See **China clay**.

Leather-hard. A stage in the drying process when the clay is no longer plastic but is damp enough for the surface to be textured or smoothed using a tool.

Luster. A shiny metallic surface applied on an already fired glaze surface. A commercial luster was developed for use in the ceramics factories of Staffordshire during the 1700s. Transmutation luster, however, the technique used by the Isnik (Persian), Egyptian, and Hispano-Moresque potters, dates back to the ninth century and involves firing in a muffle kiln.

Once firing. A technique of combining the glaze and bisque firing. Applying glaze to unfired pottery is termed "raw" glazing.

Onglaze. A decoration or coloring technique, such as china painting or luster decoration, in which the pigments are applied to the already fired glaze surface.

Oxidation firing. A firing during which there is abundant oxygen, allowing oxides to achieve their full coloration.

Oxides. Metallic oxides, produced when oxygen chemically combines with a metal, add color to glazes. Common oxides are copper (green, pink-rose to reddish mauve when reduced), cobalt (blue), iron (yellow, to brown and black), and tin (white).

Porcelain. A white, vitrified, translucent clay body that is usually fired at 1,300° C. or above. Marco Polo is accredited with naming porcelain after a little white shell known as *porcelino* ("little pig"). This should not be confused with soft-paste porcelain and bone china, which are not true porcelains.

Press molding. A method of forming by pressing plastic clay into a plaster mold.

Raku. A Japanese technique produced during the sixteenth century that is a combination of a philosophical intent and a distinctive firing process. Pots made of a refractory clay are first bisque fired and then later glazed, decorated, and plunged into a raku kiln with tongs, to be withdrawn as soon as the glaze fluxes and thrust first into sawdust, straw, or wet grass to be reduced and finally dunked into water. The development of raku is tied to the rise of the Zen Buddhist—inspired tea ceremony, a meditative ritual. The term *raku* appropriately can be translated as "happiness." This name was bestowed upon one of the first raku potters, Chojiro, in 1598 by the ruler Hideyoshi, and the family tradition and name have continued for four centuries to the present. Raku became a popular technique in the United States in the mid-sixties.

Reduction firing. A stoneware firing technique that limits the oxygen supply and results in color changes of both the clay body and the glaze. Clay turns darker in reduction, glazes become colder, with a tendency toward blues and greens.

Sagger (saggar). A container made of refractory clays, used to protect pottery from direct contact with the flames of the kiln during firing.

Salt glaze. A glaze created by the introduction of salt to the kiln during firing. The salt vaporizes, forming a sodium silicate glaze and a distinctive breakup or speckling on the ceramic surface.

Sang de boeuf (Fr. "bull's blood"). A copper reduction glaze that achieves a wide range of reddish colors from soft pinks to liver reds. The latter are referred to somewhat unflatteringly as "horses's liver" glazes.

Shard (sherd). A broken piece of pottery.

Slip casting. The creation of forms by pouring slip into a multipart plaster mold. The plaster absorbs the water in the clay and leaves behind the clay. When this has dried sufficiently, the mold is removed. This technique allows for complex forms, thin-walled vessels, and sharp ornamental detail.

Slipwares. The generic title for wares (usually earthenware) decorated with slip under a lead glaze. Several techniques exist of applying the slip: trailing it from a container with a thin spout; feathering, the trailing of lines of slip and then drawing through them in the opposite direction; combing; and sgraffito, the incising of decoration through the slip.

Soaking. Maintaining the maximum temperature of a particular firing for a length of time to allow full penetration of the heat.

Sprigging. The attaching of low-relief ornament to the surface of a pot.

Stoneware. Pottery fired at temperatures of 1,200° C. and above. Stoneware is vitreous and does not require glazing to hold water.

Terra sigillata. A colloidal suspension of the very finest clay particles, so fine that they fuse at a lower temperature than the clay itself, providing a smooth, glazelike surface on pottery. Popular in Greek, Etruscan, and Roman pottery before the discovery of lead glaze. It fires to either red or black, depending upon whether the atmosphere is oxidation or reduction.

BIBLIOGRAPHY

The following is a general listing, by no means definitive, of books, articles, and catalogs that deal with the subject of modern American pottery and the artists represented here. An asterisk (*) at the end of an entry indicates that the reference cited contains a detailed bibliography.

GENERAL

Cincinnati Art Museum. *The Ladies God Bless 'Em.* Essay by Carol Macht, chronology by Kenneth Trapp. Cincinnati, Ohio, 1976.*

Clark, Garth. *A Century of Ceramics in the United States, 1878–1978.* Preface by Margie Hughto. New York: E. P. Dutton, 1979.*

Clark, Garth. *Ceramic Art: Comment and Review, 1872–1977.* New York: E. P. Dutton, 1978.*

Clark, Garth (ed.). *Transactions of the Ceramics Symposium: 1979.* Los Angeles: Institute for Ceramic History, 1980.*

Coplans, John. *Abstract Expressionist Ceramics.* Irvine: University of California Press, 1966.

Evans, Paul F. *Art Pottery of the United States: An Encyclopedia of Producers and Their Marks.* New York: Charles Scribner's Sons, 1974.*

Harrington, LaMar. *Ceramics in the Pacific Northwest.* Seattle: University of Washington Press, 1979.*

Nordness, Lee. *Objects USA.* New York: The Viking Press, 1970.

Rhodes, Daniel. *Pottery Form.* Radnor, Pa.: Chilton Books, 1976.

San Francisco Museum of Art. *A Decade of Ceramic Art: 1962–1972.* Essay by Suzanne Foley. San Francisco, 1975.

Scripps College. *The Fred and Mary Marer Collection.* Essays by James Melchert and Paul Soldner. Claremont, Calif., 1974.

Slivka, Rose. "The New Ceramic Presence." *Craft Horizons* 21 (July–August 1961).

RUDY AUTIO

Depew, Dave. "The Archie Bray Foundation." *Ceramics Monthly* 20 (May 1972).

Evanston Art Center. *The Ceramic Vessel as Metaphor.* Essay by Alice Westphal. Evanston, Ill., 1977.

Everson Museum of Art. *24th Ceramic National Exhibition, 1966–1968.* Syracuse, N.Y., 1968.

Kalamazoo Institute of Arts. *Contemporary Ceramics: The Artist's Viewpoint.* Kalamazoo, Mich., 1977.

Kangas, Matthew. "Rudy Autio: Massive Narrations." *American Craft* 40 (October–November 1980).

VAL CUSHING

Campbell Museum. *Soup Tureens: 1976.* Introduction by Ralph Collier, essay by Helen Williams Drutt. Camden, N.J., 1976.

"Ceramics East Coast." *Craft Horizons* 25–26 (June 1966).

Everson Museum of Art. *The Ceramic National, 1968–1970.* Syracuse, N.Y., 1970.

New Gallery. *Clay Today.* Introduction by James McKinnel, essay by Abner Jonas. Iowa City: School of Fine Arts, State University of Iowa, 1962.

WILLIAM P. DALEY

Cochran, Malcolm. *Contemporary Clay: Ten Approaches.* Hanover, N.H.: Dartmouth College, 1976.

Daley, William P. "Artist & Teacher." *School Arts,* March 1963.

Daley, William P. "Celebration of Clay." *American Craft* 39 (August–September 1979).

McTwigan, Michael. "Duality in Clay: William Daley." *American Craft* 40 (December 1980–January 1981).

Olitski, Jules. "Pots for Show." *Ceramics Monthly,* December 1956.

Philadelphia Museum of Art. *Philadelphia: Three Centuries of American Art.* Philadelphia, 1976.

RICHARD DEVORE

Artner, Alan G. "Ceramics: From Craft to Class." *Chicago Tribune,* February 8, 1976.

Colby, Joy H. "Sculpture by Another Name." *Detroit News,* January 22, 1978.

Donohoe, Victoria. "Major Ceramic Artist Keeps Things Fundamental." *Philadelphia Inquirer,* December 30, 1976.

Jones, Kenneth W. "Richard E. DeVore." *Philadelphia Arts Exchange* 1 (March–April 1977).

Kline, Katy. "Pots, Paintings: A Common Thread." *Courier Express* (Buffalo, N.Y.), April 1978.

Mehring, Howard. "Richard DeVore." *Washington Review,* December 1977–January 1978.

Miro, Marsha. "What Makes Art out of a Pottery Bowl." *Detroit Free Press,* January 22, 1978.

Nasisse, Andy. "The Ceramic Vessel as Metaphor." *New Art Examiner*, January, 1976.

"A Potter Called DeVore." *The Cranbrook Magazine*, Fall 1972.

KEN FERGUSON

Melcher, Victoria Kirsch. "Tradition and Vitality: The Ceramics of Ken Ferguson." *American Craft* 39 (January 1980).

New Gallery. *Clay Today*. Introduction by James McKinnel, essay by Abner Jonas. Iowa City: School of Fine Arts, State University of Iowa, 1962.

Sewalt, Charlotte. "An Interview with Kenneth Ferguson." *Ceramics Monthly* 26 (February 1978).

MICHAEL FRIMKESS

Frimkess, Michael. "The Importance of Being Classical." *Craft Horizons* 25–26 (March–April 1966).

McChesney, Mary Fuller. "Michael Frimkess and the Cultured Pot." *Craft Horizons* 33 (December 1973).

JOHN GLICK

Broner, R. "Exhibitions." *Craft Horizons* 27 (January–February 1967).

Glick, John. "The Extruder As a Design Tool: An Expanded Usage." *Studio Potter* 7 (1978).

Glick, John. "Studio Dinnerware." *Ceramics Monthly* 27 (December 1979).

Glick, John. "Studio Management." *Studio Potter*, Summer 1973 and Winter 1973–74.

Kansas City Art Institute. *Eight Independent Production Potters*. Kansas City, Mo., 1976.

Omega Workshop. Catalog. Introduction by Roger Fry. London, ca. 1914.

Shafer, Tom. "John Glick." *Ceramics Monthly* 20 (September 1972).

Shafer, Tom. *The Professional Potter.* New York: Watson-Guptill Publications, 1978.

Sun Valley Center for the Arts. *The Studio Potter: A Question of Quality.* Edited by Jim Romberg. Sun Valley, Idaho, 1979.

Syracuse University. *New Works in Clay II.* Essay by Garth Clark. Syracuse, N.Y.: Joe and Emily Lowe Art Gallery, 1978.

KAREN KARNES

American Crafts Council. *Salt Glazed Ceramics.* New York, 1972.

Robertson, Seonaid. "Karen Karnes." *Ceramic Review*, March–April 1978.

Schwartz, Judith S. "The Essential Karnes." In *Karen Karnes: Works, 1964–1977.* New York: Hadler Gallery, 1977.

Smith, Dido. "Karen Karnes." *Craft Horizons* 18 (May–June 1958).

WARREN MACKENZIE

Kalamazoo Institute of Arts. *Contemporary Ceramics: The Artist's Viewpoint.* Kalamazoo, Mich., 1977.

Reeve, John. "Warren MacKenzie and the Straight Pot." *Craft Horizons* 36 (June 1976).

Schwartz, Judith S. "Tureens: Soup's In." *Craft Horizons* 36 (April 1976).

RON NAGLE

Brown, Sylvia. "The Tough and Tender Look of Ron Nagle's New Wares." In *Ron Nagle: 1978 Adaline Kent Award Exhibition.* San Francisco: San Francisco Art Institute, 1978.

Felton, David. "Nagle among the Termites." *Rolling Stone*, August 24, 1978.

Halverstadt, Hal. "Ron Nagle in Rock and Glass." *Craft Horizons* 31 (June 1971).

Pugliese, Joseph. "Ron Nagle the Potter." *Craft Horizons* 31 (June 1971).

McDonald, Robert. "New Work by Ron Nagle." *Artweek*, November 22, 1975.

KENNETH PRICE

Coplans, John. "The Sculpture of Kenneth Price." *Art International* 8 (March 20, 1964).

Derfner, Phyllis. "Kenneth Price at Willard." *Art in America* 63 (May–June 1975).

Hopkins, Henry T. "Kenneth Price: Untitled Ceramic." *Artforum* 2 (August 1963).

King, Mary. "Ceramics Exhibit by Kenneth Price." *St. Louis Post-Dispatch*, October 3, 1976.

Layton, Peter. "Kenneth Price Cups at Kasmin." *Studio International* 179 (February 1970).

Lippard, Lucy C. "Kenneth Price." In *Kenneth Price, Robert Irwin.* Los Angeles: Los Angeles County Museum, 1966.

Parks, Addison. Exhibition review. *Arts* (January 1980).

Radcliff, Carter. "Notes on Small Sculpture." *Artforum* 14 (April 1976).

Russell, John. "Kenneth Price." *The New York Times*, December 7, 1979.

Simon, Joan. "An Interview with Kenneth Price." *Art in America* 68 (January 1980).

Tuchman, Maurice. *Kenneth Price: Happy's Curios.* Los Angeles: Los Angeles County Museum, 1978.

JERRY ROTHMAN

Beard, Geoffrey W. *Modern Ceramics.* London: Studio Vista, 1969.

Campbell Museum. *Soup Tureens: 1976.* Essay by Helen Drutt. Camden, N.J., 1976.

"Jerry Rothman." *Ceramics Monthly*, November 1976.

Vanguard Gallery. *Bauhaus-Baroque.* Essay by Garth Clark. Claremont, Calif.: Ceramic Arts Library, 1978.

Victoria and Albert Museum. *20 American Studio Potters.* London, 1966.

PAUL SOLDNER

"Ceramics: West Coast." *Craft Horizons* 25–26 (July 1966).

Levin, Elaine. "Portfolio: Paul Soldner." *Ceramics Monthly* 27 (June 1979).

Scripps College. *The Fred and Mary Marer Collection.* Essays by James Melchert and Paul Soldner. Claremont, Calif., 1974.

Soldner, Paul. "Raku As I Know It." *Ceramic Review*, April 1973.

RUDOLF STAFFEL

Clark, Garth. "The Contradictory Chiaroscuro of Rudolf Staffel." In *Rudolf Staffel.* Philadelphia: Helen Drutt Gallery, 1980.

Cochran, Malcolm. *Contemporary Clay: Ten Approaches.* Hanover, N.H.: Dartmouth College, 1976.

Victoria and Albert Museum. *20 American Studio Potters.* London, 1966.

Winokur, Paula and Robert. "The Light of Rudolf Staffel." *Craft Horizons* 37 (April 1977).

SUSANNE G. STEPHENSON

Avatt, Corinne. "Ceramic Artist Makes a Forceful Statement." *Birmingham Eccentric*, September 15, 1977.

Finkel, Marilyn. "Susanne Stephenson." *Craft Horizons* 38 (January 1978).

New Gallery. *Clay Today.* Introduction by James McKinnel, essay by Abner Jonas. Iowa City: School of Fine Arts, State University of Iowa, 1962.

TOSHIKO TAKAEZU

Brown, Conrad. "Toshiko Takaezu." *Craft Horizons* 19–20 (March–April 1956).

Hoffman, J.; Driscole, D.; and Zahler, M. C. A. *A Study in Regional Taste: The May Show, 1919–1975.* Essay by Jay Hoffman, preface by G. Weisberg. Cleveland: Cleveland Museum of Art, 1977.

Hurley, Joseph. "Excellence: Toshiko Takaezu." *American Craft* 39 (October–November 1979).

New Jersey State Museum. *Toshiko Takaezu.* Introduction by Joan Mondale. Trenton, N.J., 1979.

Pyron, Bernard. "The Tao and Dada of Recent American Ceramic Art." *Artforum* 2 (March 1964).

ROBERT TURNER

Duberman, Martin. *Black Mountain: An Exploration of Community.* New York: E. P. Dutton, 1972.

Nicholas, Donna. "The Ceramic Nationals at Syracuse." *Craft Horizons* 32 (December 1972).

Rhodes, Daniel. "Robert Turner." *Craft Horizons* 17–18 (May–June 1979).

Shapiro, Howard Yana. "I Love You Bob Turner." *Craft Horizons* 32 (August 1972).

PETER VOULKOS

Ashton, Dore. *Modern American Sculpture.* New York: Harry Abrams, 1967.

Brown, Conrad. "Peter Voulkos." *Craft Horizons* 27 (October 1956).

Fisher, H. "Art of Peter Vouklos," *Artforum* 17 (November 1978).

Levin, Elaine. "Peter Voulkos: A Retrospective, 1948–1978." *Artweek*, March 18, 1978.

Levin, Elaine. "Portfolio: Peter Voulkos." *Ceramics Monthly* 24 (November 1978).

Melchert, James. "Peter Voulkos: A Return to Pottery." *Craft Horizons* 28 (September–October 1968).

The Museum of Modern Art. *Peter Voulkos.* New York, 1960.

Slivka, Rose. "The New Clay Drawings of Peter Voulkos." *Craft Horizons* 34 (October 1974).

Slivka, Rose. *Peter Voulkos: A Dialogue with Clay.* New York: New York Graphic Society, 1978.

BEATRICE WOOD

All India Handicrafts Board. *Ceramics by Beatrice Wood.* New Delhi, 1961.

Bryan, Robert. "The Ceramics of Beatrice Wood." *Craft Horizons* 30 (April 1970).

Hapgood, E. R. "All the Cataclysms: A Brief Survey of the Life of Beatrice Wood." *Arts Magazine* 52 (June 1977).

Hare, Denise. "The Lustrous Life of Beatrice Wood." *Craft Horizons* 38 (June 1976).

Lovoos, Janice. "An Extraordinary Craftsman." *Southwest Art* 5 (April 1979).

Phoenix Art Museum. *Beatrice Wood: A Retrospective.* Foreword by Robert L. Frankl. Phoenix, Ariz., 1973.

Wood, Beatrice. "I Shock Myself." *Arts Magazine* 51 (May 1977).

BETTY WOODMAN

Clark, Garth. "Betty Woodman: The Storm in a Teacup." In *Betty Woodman.* Rochester, Minn.: Rochester Art Center, 1980.

DeVore, Richard. "Ceramics of Betty Woodman." *Craft Horizons* 38 (February 1978).

Kansas City Art Institute. *Eight Independent Production Potters.* Kansas City, Mo., 1976.

Woodman, Betty. "About Pots." *Decade*, February 1979.

INDEX

Page numbers in italics indicate illustrations.

Edited by Michael McTwigan
Designed by Jay Anning
Production by Lesley Poliner
Set in 11 point Century Old Style